A Year with New England's Birds

P9-CEX-517

A Year with New England's Birds

A Guide to Twenty-five Field Trips

Sandy Mallett / With illustrations by Gail Reyna

 New Hampshire Publishing Company   Somersworth

To my friend Mary Jones
who shares my joy in the woods

ISBN hardbound: 0-912274-91-3
ISBN softbound: 0-912274-87-5
Library of Congress Catalog Card Number: 77-26352
© 1978 by Sandy Mallett
Printed in the United States of America

Photograph on page 65 by Mark Mallett; all other photographs
by the author
Designed by David Ford

Acknowledgments

This book is a journal of my wanderings through some of New England's premier birding areas, but in a book such as this one, the professionals who comment and correct are essential. The expertise of Leslie Corey, Jr., Marcia Litchfield, Evan Ellison, Don McKenna, and Lee Gardiner guided me through the thicket of bird facts. The Audubon societies of each New England state were particularly helpful both in advising me of locations to visit and in opening their reference libraries to me.

I am also indebted to many friends. Bertie Weeks loaned me her incredible reference library and welcomed me to the warmth of her home, even with my cries of despair. The Bluebirds, a long-established birding club in East Rochester, New Hampshire, introduced me to Bertie and to others who gave of themselves: Helen and Ray Spinney, Vi Staley, Buffy Hescock, and Vera Bickford. I am especially grateful to Gail Reyna, who drew the gorgeous illustrations; to Bob Brown, who gave me step-by-step instructions on the use of a camera; and to my editor, Cathy Baker.

Special applause goes to my family: my husband, Norm, who has always loved the woods; my sons, Dave and Mark, who are learning to tread softly in the wilds; and my father, Rob Bogert, who started it all by introducing me to the wonders of the woods at an impressionable age.

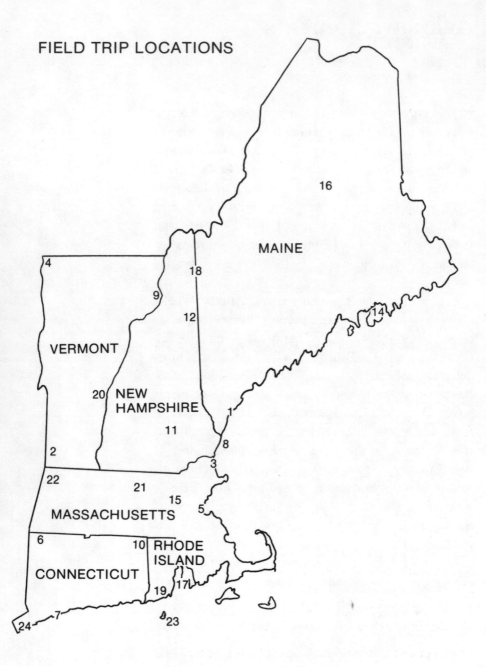

FIELD TRIP LOCATIONS

MAINE

16

VERMONT

4

18

9

12

14

NEW
HAMPSHIRE

20

1

11

8

2

3

22

21

MASSACHUSETTS

15

5

6

10

RHODE
ISLAND

CONNECTICUT

19

17

7

24

23

Contents

Introduction

A chickadee lights on our hair as we sit quietly under a tree, and, just for an instant, we become part of another world, for the freedom of birds is a vicarious freedom for humans. Our wondrous civilization gives us much, but the joy of nature reaches deep. The springy feel of moss is as sensuous as a Persian rug; the rich smell of a salt marsh is as satisfying as the aroma of freshly baked bread; the delicate ladyfern fronds are as fine as Belgian lace. And the sound of a flock of geese, a **V** in the sunset, is the music of the spheres.

In reality, of course, needs dictate to birds, as they do to us. While birds can be found in any habitat that provides them with their necessities — food, water, shelter, and nesting space — particular birds fit into particular niches. In New England birds are found everywhere, from cities to lake shores, from mountaintops to beneath the surface of the sea, from salt marshes to deep, dark forests. Along the coast, for instance, gulls scavenge at the high-water line, sandpipers run from the frothy edge of the incoming tide, and grebes dive beneath the waves some fifteen feet off shore. In the deep woods, a golden eagle soars high in the sky, a sentinel crow sits on the top branch of the tallest tree, a rose-breasted grosbeak serenades from a limb twenty feet off the ground, a yellowthroat stares curiously from a bush, and a towhee scratches in the leaves lying below. A crossbill's special beak permits it to find food in the relatively sterile habitat of a coniferous forest; the phoebe's lack of fear allows it to nest near human habitation.

Because birds' habits and habitats change as the months go by, the variety of birds we are able to see in any one place depends in part on the season. In winter, resident birds' full attention is on food and shelter.

1

Since their metabolism is so high, they must eat a lot and often. (This is why backyard feeders are more attractive to birds in the winter.) Many of New England's winter birds have migrated here from even further north to replace the summer residents who have left for lands as far away as South America, where food supplies are more readily available.

Spring migration starts very early in South America. The birds hit storms and cold along the way, yet often arrive in the same nesting territory during the same week year after year. New England has two major migratory routes: the Atlantic and the Hudson River flyways (the latter includes Lake Champlain). Spring is also the easiest time to sight birds, since their mating habits make them highly visible; males sing, and some dance, to attract mates and establish a territory. As pairs nest and begin to raise their young, they become more secretive.

Summer finds most birds flying free and teaching their young the facts of life. Now their bright breeding plumage molts to a duller rendition for camouflage (making identification, even for experienced birders a frustrating experience), and their songs are largely replaced by scattered notes and calls.

Come autumn, those birds that are not year round residents prepare for the fall migration. Many more birds are flying south than will return in the spring. For birders, this is a sad time.

How to Use This Book

The twenty-five field trips in this book describe just a few of the innumerable birding areas available to the public in New England. Although this selection includes some very special places known for their birdlife, it is also representative of the varied habitats New England has to offer. Most birds that forage in Vermont's Woodford Park, for example, can be expected to show up throughout northern New England's woodlands. And because the birds that inhabit a particular place vary over the course of a year, I have geared the excursions to particular months. For each walk, hike, canoe trip, and boat trip, I have generally tried to describe not only the habitat but also the birds that you can hope to see, or hear, and any habits they may be displaying. Many birds, of course, can be found in several habitats; by using the Bird Index the casual or beginning birder should be able to assemble a more complete picture of any given bird, as I have mentioned the different behaviors of some birds at the most appropriate time. Some birds mentioned are habitually there; others were exciting for their rarity.

For each trip, I have also included a check-list of birds it is possible to find at that place during the season discussed. These lists were compiled from sanctuary or Audubon Society check-lists for that area whenever possible, the word of the resident naturalist, or, as a last resort, field guide maps of bird ranges. However, since bird territories are not absolutely stable, it is possible to spot a bird that is not on the list. Within the lists the birds are arranged by family. The scientific family in some instances has been further broken down for clarity's sake. For example, the family *Fringillidae* includes, but shows separate listings for, buntings, finches, sparrows, and towhees. The common names are those used in *The Audubon Society Field Guide to North America, Eastern Region,* which are based on the 1957 edition of the American Ornithologist's Union's *Check-list of North American Birds* as revised through 1976. The accepted common names of a few birds have changed over the years (the Baltimore oriole is now called the northern oriole and the sparrow hawk, the American kestrel), and in those instances I have included the former name in parentheses.

This book is not meant to be a field guide and should be used in conjunction with one. Roger Tory Peterson's *A Field Guide to the Birds,* Golden Press's *Birds of North America,* and *The Audubon Society Field Guide to North American Birds* are all worthwhile investments. Neither is this book a detailed trail guide. Part of the adventure of searching for birds is the wandering about. Maps for many of these places are available at the park or sanctuary headquarters. For some of the backwoods trails, local sporting goods stores carry hiking guides and the Appalachian Mountain Club and United States Geological Survey topographic maps.

The Appendix lists, by state and habitat, other bird sites in New England worth exploring. It is my hope that this book will stimulate your interest in hiking and birding.

Notes for Beginning Birders

Take your time! Birding excursions cannot be successful if they are viewed as ground-gaining hikes where distance is all important. Remember that slow, quiet movement is interpreted by birds as "natural and not dangerous." (This is why cats are so successful.)

The list of equipment necessary for a birder is remarkably short. Always bring your field guide. It gives a color illustration or photograph, the general habitat, description, size, and voice of each bird that can be found in the region. Some also map each bird's usual range and describe its characteristic habits.

A set of binoculars is also important. Many birders use 7x35 or 8x40 binoculars (the 7x and 8x refer to the number of times an image is magnified and the 35 and 40 to the width in millimeters of the lenses). The wider field of 7x35s makes finding a flitting bird easier than if you use the more powerful 8x40s. A lightweight set is appreciated after a day's use. I recommend an inexpensive set, since you will use it in all sorts of weather (and perhaps leave it behind on your picnic rock). A spotting scope with a long tripod makes identification of a hawk in a high nest or a duck at sea much easier. Perhaps a group or club expenditure makes sense in this case.

If you plan to walk for any distance or length of time, you should have the usual hiker's accouterments with you: strong boots, compass, flashlight, topographical map, and canteen. A day pack will help organize all these items as well as hold your lunch. Bug dope is an absolute necessity for spring migration walks. Waving your arms around to bat black flies is a quick way to decrease bird sightings.

Overwhelming at first, bird identification can be sorted out. If you were to recognize only one bird a day you would quickly become expert. Go with a friend who knows birds. Field experience is better than any guide. A small notebook is useful for recording pertinent facts about a bird you can't readily identify; note its habitat, what it was eating, its general size, and, of course, any field marks, such as wing patches, tail bands, or eye stripes, that you pick out. As you spend more time in the field, you will develop the skill to notice identifying marks. With time you will also come to recognize different bird songs and calls, other aids to identification. You might find it useful to listen to the recordings of bird songs and calls produced by the Cornell University ornithological laboratories before venturing out in the field. Many males sing lovely mating songs all spring long. The females, however, confine their vocal activities to a dry "chip" or perhaps a musical "chirp."

The notebook you carry can also hold your life list of where, when, and how you spotted a particular bird for the first time. Birders traveled from all over America to Newburyport, Massachusetts, to record Ross' gull on their life lists a few years ago. It was the first time this bird had been seen in America south of Point Barrow, Alaska, a place few people would have a chance to visit. A rare life bird is a soul-stirring thrill, but the gentle, common chickadee provides the warmth needed in everyday living.

1 January on Marginal Way

[NORTHERN COAST]

Close to the cliffs of the Marginal Way sea birds ride waves churned by yesterday's nor'easter. We chose this particular day to walk the mile-long path in Ogunquit, Maine, in hopes of sighting a few birds that normally spend their winter far out to sea. The storm may have driven them to the land's edge.

Lobster traps are piled high on the wharves of Perkins Cove, where we park. The herring gulls are always here, circling, expecting. Flocks of gulls, both herring and the larger black-backed, follow the fishermen on their rounds, knowing that unwanted fish in the catch are pitched into the sea and are then "easy pickin's."

We start up the paved walkway on the cove's ocean side by a rocky beach. Pieces of lobster trap, weathered pearl gray by salt water and rubbed to interesting shapes by grinding stones, mark the high tide line. The pavement, a boon to wheelchair birders in most weather, is

7

icy today, but the friendly greetings of fellow walkers are not.

At the top of the cliff we set up our spotting scope and slowly scan the ocean. To the naked eye, only a few scattered birds show, but with the scope we see hundreds!

Near shore two red-breasted mergansers swim side by side. We blink our eyes, and they are gone. They have dived through a wave in pursuit of fish. They use both their webbed feet and their wings to swim underwater. Fifty yards away the female and then the male bob up. Their crests ruffle in the steady, cold wind. These large crests, the brown chest patch of the male, and the lack of contrast between the throat and head of the female distinguish them from the common mergansers, who also frequent this coastline in the winter. The common's smaller crests are barely noticeable.

Large rafts of black and white oldsquaw ducks checker the water to our left. Their needlelike tails puncture the sky as they crest a wave. They ride high in the water, unlike the white-winged scoter swimming nearby.

Floating so close to the wave-battered cliffs that we hold our breaths are a pair of common eiders. We know of these ducks because of their famous down, the soft underfeathers that are used to fill pillows and coverlets. Eiders nest on some of the outlying islands of Maine, but there are few such convenient places to see them as here on this cliff walk. These very large black and white ducks dine well on clams, mussels, sea urchins, and crabs. Because of their size, they appear awkward in flight as the flocks travel in lines just a few feet above the water.

Winter Birds
Marginal Way

Alcids: dovekie (rarely)
Cormorants: great
Ducks: bufflehead, common eider, common goldeneye, common scoter, greater scaup, oldsquaw, red-breasted merganser, surf scoter, white-winged scoter
Grebes: horned, red-necked
Gulls: great black-backed, herring, ring-billed
Loons: common, red-throated
Sandpipers: dunlin, purple

Numerous inland winter birds also frequent the Marginal Way.

As we continue the breathtaking walk along the cliffs (breathtaking both for its beauty and the cold), we catch sight of a tiny bufflehead duck almost lost in the immensity of the waves. The water beats at the immovable granite, foaming at the mouth of an inlet. Mackerel fishermen cast off these rocks in the spring, but only the gulls venture out on them now.

Around the corner a whitewashed lighthouse overlooks a shell beach in a cove. Limpet, moon snail, periwinkle, blue mussel, and clamshells have been hammered into multicolored sand. A gull wheels round and round overhead, lines up his target of hard-packed sand, and releases his missile — a clam. It hits dead center and cracks open. The gull drops like a helicopter and gulps down the contents before others can grab his meal.

Protected by a rock outcropping, this small cove is a harbor of refuge. A pair of common goldeneye ducks is resting. The white patch of his cheek is smaller than the white head patch of the male bufflehead, although the ducks are otherwise similar in color. We know that the courtship of the goldeneye is early in the year but are surprised when he displays for her today. He raises his head until it almost touches his back, pointing his bill to the sky, and calls a most unmelodious note. She finds it glorious; we don't. As he takes off, the whistling of his wings startles us.

Normally the dovekie waits out the winter far offshore by the fishing banks, but the blustery nor'easter has blown a pair close to the cliffs. This "robin of the ocean" can weather any storm way out to sea, but sometimes the relentless wind will drive one over land where, exhausted, he will light and soon die. With legs set far back, the dovekie is a first-class swimmer, but their position does not allow him sufficient thrust to take off from land. These two seem fine as they whirl in the water like wind-up toys in a tub at a country fair.

Wet-suited surfers perform like seals where the river meets the ocean — wild rides today. We turn to leave as a gull's piercing cry raises our hair. How right is this sound in the chill of the wind. Hot clam broth from a thermos warms our bodies, and the success of the day warms our spirit.

Bufflehead

2 February in Woodford Park

[NORTHERN WOODLANDS]

"Snowbirds" flutter through the brush of Woodford State Park as we strap on our snowshoes for a winter walk around Adams Reservoir. The park entrance on VT 9, only 11½ miles east of Bennington, is kept clear by highway crews all winter. Because the park is close to many of Vermont's famous downhill ski areas, inns are available for overnight accommodations.

The trail circling the reservoir is about two miles long, winding through a second-growth mix of hardwood, fir, and spruce. It is marked by blue blazes, with two, one above the other, indicating a change in direction. Needless to say, we wouldn't try this woodland trek in February without either snowshoes or cross-country skis. We would sink out of sight!

As we climb to the side of the snow-clad hill, we look down through the skeletons of leafless trees to the open expanse of Adams Reservoir. A gray and white flock

11

ripples across the openings, eating seeds from the tips of tall grasses where the bushes have kept the snow shallow. Dark-eyed juncos are the "snowbirds" of New England. These friendly little birds summer in Canada and move "south" for the winter. They flit from their seed gathering to a nearby road to pick at fine gravel, which is necessary for their digestion. The quickest way to identify them as they fly across a gray sky is by the white outer edges of their tail feathers.

A hairy woodpecker works on a nearby oak limb trying to dig out a borer. The hairy is larger than the very similar downy, the most common woodpecker of the East, but much more shy. In winter, however, he seems to lose much of his fear and is frequently seen pecking at suet balls on feeders. He responds when we imitate him by tapping with a stick on a tree trunk.

Do you wonder how a woodpecker knows where to drill to find a grub under the tree bark? One theory has him striking the tree and resting his bill in the hole to feel vibrations from a working grub. (I've never seen one resting in this manner, however.) Another theory holds that he sounds for hollow spots where the grub has tunneled, as we sound for studs in the house by tapping with a hammer on the wall. A third theory, currently accepted by many ornithologists, is that he actually hears the grub as it bores away.

The jumbled boulders of a spring runoff have become snow-covered giants crouching close to the trail. Snowshoe rabbit tracks appear from beneath a fallen log. We notice that the large hind feet land in the snow in front of the smaller forefeet. Tracking on a warm sunshiny day-after-a-blizzard tells us many stories, for after being snowed in for a day, the birds and animals all come out of their shelters to feed.

We see where a red squirrel has broken into his cache of seeds and unwittingly spilled some at the base of a large maple. Tiny bird tracks surround the area — perhaps the juncos again, or chickadees. Another snowbank shows a hole and wing prints where a ruffed grouse, or partridge as it is called in New England, has burst free after lying protected from the storm. The

February
Woodford Park

grouse dived into the snow at the start of the blizzard to emerge only where the warmth of the sunlight attracted it. If a warm front had turned the snow to sleet, a crust would have formed, trapping the bird in its sanctuary. After a winter of ice storms, few ruffed grouse are left to "bud" (eat quaking aspen buds) come early spring.

We clump down the woods trail and into the open, a bog in the summer, where more prints tell a clear story. From beneath a partly decayed stump a mouse began a foraging trip. His minute footprints, separated by the shallow trench of a tail print, head straight for a tangle of grass, both food and cover. A rush of wings must have alerted him to danger, for the prints suddenly veer one way and then another as he frantically dodges. And there — a tremendous impact in the snow: wide wing prints, deep chest print, spread tail print, and even talon prints. No blood. But look! The mouse footprints continue to a hole by a tuft of grass. A near miss.

Perhaps it was a snowy owl who tried for the mouse. This arctic bird regularly winters in New England when his usual food supply of lemmings declines on the tundra of the far north. Or possibly it was a red-shouldered hawk trying to eke out a living, precarious at this time of year. When soaring, this hawk can be told by the translucent "window" near the tips of his wings. When in a tree fixing up last year's nest, his red shoulders identify him.

As we complete the circuit the silence of the winter woods is broken by tiny squeaks from a flock of black-

February
Woodford Park

Winter Birds
Woodford Park

Chickadees: black-capped, boreal
Creeper: brown
Crows: common
Falcons: American kestrel (sparrow hawk)
Finches: American goldfinch, pine siskin, purple finch, red crossbill, white-winged crossbill
Grosbeaks: evening, pine
Grouse: ruffed, spruce
Hawks: goshawk, red-tailed, sharp-shinned

Jays: blue
Kinglets: golden-crowned
Nuthatches: red-breasted, white-breasted
Owls: great horned, hawk (rarely), long-eared, saw-whet, screech, snowy (rarely)
Shrikes: northern
Sparrows: dark-eyed (slate-colored) junco, fox, song, swamp, tree
Starling: starling
Woodpeckers: downy, hairy, northern three-toed (rarely)

capped chickadees, kinglets, a lone boreal chickadee, and a brown creeper. The acrobats swing from the hemlock trapeze, while the brown creeper works up the tree trunk in a dizzying spiral.

We perform our own gymnastics going back to the car as the soft snow catches the tips of our snowshoes.

February
Woodford Park

Dark-eyed junco

3 March on Plum Island

[NORTHERN COAST/ATLANTIC FLYWAY]

We pack the Coleman stove in the car along with a New England boiled dinner and jelly beans, dress in our warmery, and take off on our annual Easter parade to Plum Island. Our goal today is the Canada geese; the fertile salt marsh in the island's lee is one of their coastal feeding grounds.

Behind Plum Island off Newburyport, Massachusetts, the mouth of the Merrimack River also lies protected from Atlantic storms. The sea ducks are everywhere in this sheltered bay: buffleheads, scoters, and oldsquaws float alone and in rafts of hundreds. The overlooks are filled with cars of birders bundled to their noses.

We drive past the local airport, forcing ourselves to continue rather than pull over to watch the many grazing geese. Finally we arrive at the boundary of Parker River National Wildlife Refuge, which covers the southernmost six miles of Plum Island. "Live Parking for Nature Study" signs welcome the in-car birder. No

15

longer are we obstructing traffic when we stop to watch a few geese only fifteen feet away. After eyeing us, they return to their feeding in this marvelously rich marsh. Their necks bend gracefully. Their white chin straps hold heads alert as we start the car.

Hellcat Swamp Trail, our destination, begins at parking lot 6. This mile and a half long self-guiding boardwalk trail winds through a freshwater swamp, marsh grasslands, and one of the last wild barrier beaches in the northeast.

Close at hand a ring-necked pheasant jumps from a thicket of greenbriers as we close the car door. Then a green-winged teal squeals up from a pothole. Open water has tempted him to stay here all winter. Each small pothole supports ducks. The most common ducks of New England, blacks, float in most of them. The large blacks are sooty gray but not black. Sweet fern scents the air as we brush past.

Crossing the road, we walk the dunes first. There is little bird movement here on the ocean side. The roar of heavy surf surges over the crests of grassy dunes. The delicate dune vegetation holds most of the sand in place, and the boardwalk protects the vegetation from man's crushing feet. It also makes easier walking over the soft sand.

"Eenk, ong, awk, awk." Overhead a flock of geese talk. Mixed with the Canadas are a few snows. These

March
Plum Island

Spring Birds
Plum Island

Buntings: snow
Chickadees: black-capped
Cormorants: double-crested, great
Crows: common
Ducks: American wigeon, Barrow's goldeneye, black, blue-winged teal, bufflehead, canvasback, common eider, common goldeneye, common scoter, Eurasian wigeon (rarely), gadwall, greater scaup, green-winged teal, harlequin, hooded merganser, king eider (rarely), mallard, northern shoveler, oldsquaw, pintail, red-breasted merganser, redhead, ring-necked, ruddy, surf scoter, tufted (rarely), white-winged scoter, wood
Eagles: bald (rarely)
Falcons: American kestrel (sparrow hawk), merlin (pigeon hawk), peregrine
Finches: American goldfinch, purple
Gannet: gannet
Geese: brant, Canada, snow (blue)
Grebes: horned, pied-billed, red-necked
Grosbeaks: evening, rose-breasted
Gulls: Bonaparte's, great black-backed, herring, Iceland, ring-billed

16

greater snow geese are an eastern race and nest in Labrador and Baffin Island. Most make their migration directly from their wintering grounds to their breeding areas in one uninterrupted flight several thousand feet up. The few we see here are probably immatures making the return flight for the first time.

We cross over to the marsh portion of the trail. Twisted cedars are haunts for a few wintering sparrows, yellow-rumped warblers, mockingbirds, and cedar waxwings. A white-throated sparrow shows off his elegant head. More common is the flock of snow buntings on the dike. They come south with the winter winds from the most northerly lands and are attracted to open places such as farm fields or grassy dunes along the coast. Their swirling is so like a snow flurry, we look to the darkening sky.

A hot Easter dinner is a welcome break in the middle of this cold beach day. Refreshed, we head with binoculars to the blind. "Quiet, please," says a polite sign. The ducks quack and then make their little grunting noises as they turn to eat. We peek through the slots in the blind at the pothole beyond and spy a flock of mallards. Green heads glow. A patch toward the backs of the wings is iridescent blue. This patch, or speculum, sets off most of the surface-feeding ducks, both male and female, from the diving ducks. A female tips tail up, dabbling for tender roots.

March
Plum Island

Hawks: Cooper's, goshawk, marsh, red-shouldered, red-tailed (other species rarely)
Herons: American bittern, black-crowned night, cattle egret, glossy ibis, great blue, great (common) egret, green, least bittern, little blue, snowy egret, yellow-crowned night (rarely)
Jays: blue
Lark: horned
Loons: common, red-throated
Osprey: osprey
Pheasant: ring-necked
Plovers: American golden (rarely), black-bellied, killdeer, piping, ruddy turnstone, semipalmated

Rails: American coot, clapper, common gallinule, sora, Virginia
Sandpipers: dunlin, greater yellowlegs, least, lesser yellowlegs, pectoral, sanderling, semipalmated, short-billed dowitcher, solitary, spotted
Snipe: common
Sparrows: common redpoll, dark-eyed (slate-colored) junco, fox, house, Lapland longspur, savannah, seaside, sharp-tailed, song, swamp, tree, white-crowned, white-throated
Starling: starling
Terns: Arctic, black, Caspian (rarely), common, least, roseate

Nearby a pair of Canada geese nibble at the grass, looking quite content with their lot. Canadas mate for life. Most nest on the spongy grasslands of northern North America. While the female incubates the clutch of eggs, the male defends her. As anyone who has faced a hissing, wing-rapping goose can testify, his is a strong defense! There is no defense, however, against one predator of chicks born in a New England nest, the snapping turtle. Swimming underwater, he grabs one from below. Surprisingly, bass also take a large toll of geese and duck young here. Today these two geese are intent only on feeding, not on the future of their kind. (How easy it is to fall into the trap of anthropomorphic thoughts.)

We leave the blind and continue the marsh walk. Plumes of phragmite grasses wave overhead as the first flakes of snow begin to fall. The walk plunges deep into the cattail marshes. In a few weeks early migrating black-crowned night herons and rails will hide here.

We climb the observation tower. The wind blows stinging bites of snow into our eyes; we see little now. The flocks have settled into the lees of dikes to wait out this final spring storm. We climb down, run quickly to the car, and head home.

March
Plum Island

Canada goose

18

4 April in Missisquoi Refuge

[NORTHERN WOODLANDS/HUDSON FLYWAY]

The spring migration of the ducks and geese is in full swing. We strain for a view of open sky as we pass through the folds of the Green Mountains and head for Missisquoi Refuge in the northwest corner of Vermont. How different it is after we reach the Lake Champlain Islands where great fields border the flatness of the lake; only silos and steeples pierce the sky.

From the bridges that connect the islands we watch trailing **Vs** approach from the southern sky. The geese are tired. No longer is their flight steady; they seem almost to tumble from the sky, they wobble and compensate so.

Missisquoi National Wildlife Refuge on VT 78 encompasses over five thousand acres. Set aside as a resting spot for migratory birds using the Hudson River flyway, the reservation includes public nature trails, jeep trails, and boat launching ramps. North Hero, a typically well-run Vermont state campground, opens in April — in time for our first-of-the-year-campout.

19

After stopping at the refuge headquarters for a map and a chat, we put the canoe in the Missisquoi River and enjoy a leisurely paddle on still waters. How good to see the ducks and geese nibbling the tender sprouts of the aquatic plants that grow here in such profusion. A night with plenty of good food and rest at this, one of their last stopovers before they get to their nesting sloughs on the Canada tundra, will completely revive them. Birds travel from hundreds to thousands of miles on their spring and fall migrations. It is remarkable how well they survive.

A pair of pintail ducks springs into the air as we round a bend in the river. Even if we were clinging to a floating log covered with camouflaging reeds instead of sitting in this yellow canoe, they would still flush! Any unusual object alarms them. Their silhouettes against the sky are sleek as they swiftly disappear around a bend. Pintails are nearly as large as the more widely known mallards and equally as beneficial, eating dragonflies, mosquitoes, water bugs, and weed seeds, along with their usual diet of plantlife. They head north as soon as they can find open water and return south early in the fall along with the blue-winged teal.

April
Missisquoi Refuge

Spring Birds
Missisquoi Refuge

Blackbirds: brown-headed cowbird, common grackle, eastern meadowlark, red-winged, rusty
Bluebirds: eastern
Buntings: indigo, snow
Chickadees: black-capped
Crows: common
Ducks: American wigeon, black, blue-winged teal, bufflehead, common goldeneye, common merganser, gadwall, green-winged teal, hooded merganser, mallard, northern shoveler, pintail, ring-necked, ruddy, scaup, wood
Eagles: bald
Falcons: American kestrel (sparrow hawk), merlin (pigeon hawk)
Finches: American goldfinch, pine siskin, purple

Flycatchers: eastern phoebe, eastern wood pewee, great crested, least, olive-sided
Geese: brant, Canada, snow (blue)
Goatsuckers: common nighthawk, whip-poor-will
Grebes: horned, pied-billed, red-necked
Grosbeaks: evening, pine, rose-breasted
Grouse: gray partridge, ruffed
Gulls: Bonaparte's, herring, ring-billed
Hawks: broad-winged, Cooper's, marsh, red-shouldered, red-tailed, sharp-shinned
Herons: American bittern, black-crowned night, great blue, green, least bittern
Hummingbirds: ruby-throated
Jays: blue
Kingbirds: eastern
Kingfishers: belted
Lark: horned
Loons: common

The name "Missisquoi" is a version of the Abasaki Indian word meaning "land of much waterfowl and much grass." We think of this as we nose into the lush grasses and three "woodies" explode from their hiding place.

Paddling quietly back upstream, we imagine the scene a month from now when common terns, their scissor tails cutting the air, will cross the open sky. They may be joined by a black tern or two, birds that are rarely seen in New England, although they are abundant in the prairie states. A few nest here near Lake Champlain, one of their most easterly nesting sites.

Although primarily a refuge for migrating Canada geese and ducks, the reservation protects other birds and animals as well. After pulling the canoe out, we walk down the one-mile nature trail that begins at the headquarters building in search of other birds. An apartment house for purple martins, our largest swallows, sits on a pole high above the parking lot awaiting the arrival of a busy colony. Long before today's interest in birding, Indians hung hollow gourds in trees to house these insect-loving birds.

We cross the railroad tracks that connect Montreal,

April
Missisquoi Refuge

Mimics: brown thrasher, gray catbird
Nuthatches: red-breasted, white-breasted
Orioles: northern (Baltimore)
Osprey: osprey
Owls: barred, great horned, saw-whet, screech
Plovers: killdeer, semipalmated
Rails: American coot, common gallinule, sora, Virginia
Sandpipers: greater yellowlegs, lesser yellowlegs, solitary, spotted, white-rumped
Shrikes: northern
Snipe: common
Sparrows: chipping, dark-eyed (slate-colored) junco, field, fox, house, savannah, song, swamp, tree, vesper, white-crowned, white-throated
Starling: starling
Swallows: bank, barn, cliff, purple martin, tree

Tanagers: scarlet
Terns: black, common
Thrushes: American robin, hermit, Swainson's, veery, wood
Vireos: Philadelphia, red-eyed, solitary, warbling, yellow-throated
Warblers: American redstart, bay-breasted, black-and-white, Blackburnian, black-throated blue, black-throated green, Canada, Cape May, chestnut-sided, Louisiana waterthrush, magnolia, Nashville, northern waterthrush, ovenbird, yellow, yellow-rumped, yellowthroat
Waxwings: cedar
Woodcock: American
Woodpeckers: downy, hairy, pileated, yellow-bellied sapsucker, yellow-shafted flicker
Wrens: house, long-billed marsh, winter

Canada, with New England and notice the hut where feed corn is stored. On the opposite side of the path a tall wire fence prevents us from inadvertently disturbing this nesting area for ducks and geese that choose not to continue their journey north.

Following a meandering creek through a field, we watch a late fox sparrow passing north. Suddenly a black-crowned night heron flushes. When it lands in a tree how awkward it appears. Herons nest in trees, but with their long legs and necks, they look like they should topple off the branch.

Woodcock fly from underfoot, startling us every time. They crouch low to the ground in the alders and will remain hidden close to the path unless we stop walking. When we do pause they think we have spotted them, and they fly away straight up and then zigzag quickly through the trees.

Spring is the season of woodcock displays — they put on quite a show. Toward evening the male struts, lowering his wings and spreading his tail like a turkey cock. He bows to the female, rises in an erratic flight, and then, wings whistling, sings a variety of notes while he tumbles back through the air.

As we enter the woods, we see many trees that beavers have gnawed down and then abandoned. The tender branches have been removed for food, and peeled sticks are caught in the underbrush of the creek bank. A red-winged blackbird surveys his domain from atop a chewed trail sign. The rangers have been busy protecting some of the larger maples and oaks with chicken wire to discourage these overly ambitious animals.

A tall elm tree just off the path has succumbed to Dutch Elm disease. While we view this as a loss, the woodpeckers are happy. Huge holes penetrate the tree. The hammering we hear comes not from a nearby farmhouse, but from the pileated woodpecker, who is common here.

A lookout point at the trail's end does not overlook Lake Champlain as we had assumed it would but a small bit of marsh. A female duck glides silently by from over our shoulders. She is hidden immediately in the grasses. She disappears so quickly that if we tried to name her, we would only be guessing.

Pintail ducks

April
Missisquoi Refuge

5 April in Arnold Arboretum

[CITY]

Birds of surprising diversity make Arnold Arboretum their home. This incomparable garden of over six thousand *varieties* of labeled ornamental trees and shrubs serves as the backdrop for our city walk late in the month. Although most cities have large parks that attract birdlife, few are as lucky as Boston. Arnold Arboretum is a special place.

Located near the junction of US 1 and MA 203 in Jamaica Plain, the 265-acre arboretum is easy to reach by car and is just a short walk from stations on the Forest Hills and Huntington subway lines. It is very much a park for pedestrians; cars are not allowed on the grounds on weekends, and permits are required during the week.

We saunter down a roadway lined with rhododendrons about to burst into bloom. A yellow warbler's glow brightens the rich green of the leaves. Although they are the most common New England warblers, we don't often see them in a city habitat. The yellowthroat, ovenbird, and yellow are all nesting warblers in Arnold Arboretum. We are even more surprised to learn that the kestrel, red-tailed hawk, and great horned owl also nest here at times. The park is large enough to support the gray squirrels, chipmunks, and English sparrows that comprise their steady diet. As we gaze at a startling orange azalea, a squirrel swishes his tail and runs across the woodchip-lined area.

We continue up the road to Bussey Hill. A low shrub, buds just breaking open, shelters a mystery bird. Probably a warbler, the tiny gray-backed, white-bellied bird sits quivering for a full two minutes fanning an elaborate, brilliant yellow tail rimmed with black. It does not look exotic enough to have escaped from the aviary at nearby Franklin Park Zoo, but . . . we suddenly realize it's a female American redstart encouraging her suitor.

Cutting through the park, we come to the circular lattice building that houses dozens of incredibly intricate Japanese bonsai trees. High overhead a nighthawk who has arrived early this year cries, "peent, peent." The swooping flights of nighthawks are an exciting city sight. They are seldom seen resting (interestingly, when they do, they sit lengthwise on the branch of a tree). In the air the white spot on their very long wings is diagnostic. Mouths that hinge far back enable them to scoop myriad insects out of the air.

The courtship of nighthawks is aerial, in keeping with their high-flying life. In a few weeks we could watch the male as he plunges head first in a speed dive with his wings partially closed. As he nears the ground, he spreads them and turns upward abruptly, producing a resonant "boom." We wonder if their eggs will be laid on the gravel roof of the administration building. Their coloring is extremely varied, ranging from a creamy white to an olive gray splotched with brown. The mottled feathers of the nesting adult camouflage the site on a city roof as they do in the woods.

Evening light cuts through the willows at a low angle. The filmy green screen hides drifting mallards on one of the small ponds. A brown thrasher and mockingbird try to outsing each other, drowning the distant noise of city traffic.

The inquisitive, confident chickadee is the state bird for Massachusetts. We sit on a bench, coaxing one closer and closer by kissing our hands, producing a come-hither sound. The delicate touch of this totally free wild creature is a thrill.

We admire the beautiful, naturalized plantings of daffodils and tulips on a low hill. Since pesticides are used for maximum flower display and to protect the trees (after all, this *is* an arboretum), we wonder to what extent they have been responsible for the decline in insectivorous birds here. Omniverous species such as the pigeon (known to ornithologists as the rock dove), English sparrow, common grackle, mourning dove, and the ever-present starling have filled this niche. These species eat just about anything and seem to have little fear of man.

City bird walks do not have to be confined to parks.

April
Arnold Arboretum

Spring Birds
Arnold Arboretum

Blackbirds: brown-headed cowbird, common grackle, red-winged, rusty
Bluebirds: eastern
Buntings: indigo
Chickadees: black-capped
Creeper: brown
Crows: common, fish
Doves: mourning, rock (pigeon)
Ducks: black, mallard, wood
Falcons: American kestrel (sparrow hawk)
Finches: American goldfinch, house, pine siskin, purple
Flycatchers: eastern phoebe, eastern wood pewee, great crested, least
Goatsuckers: common nighthawk
Grosbeaks: cardinal, rose-breasted
Gulls: great black-backed, herring, ring-billed
Hawks: Cooper's, red-shouldered, red-tailed, sharp-shinned
Herons: black-crowned night, great blue, green
Hummingbirds: ruby-throated
Jays: blue

Kingbirds: eastern
Kingfishers: belted
Kinglets: golden-crowned, ruby-crowned
Mimics: brown thrasher, gray catbird, mockingbird
Nuthatches: white-breasted
Orioles: northern (Baltimore), orchard
Owls: great horned, screech
Pheasant: ring-necked
Sandpipers: solitary, spotted
Sparrows: chipping, field, house, savannah, song, tree, vesper
Starling: starling
Swallows: barn, rough-winged, tree
Tanagers: scarlet
Thrushes: American robin, gray-cheeked, hermit, Swainson's, wood, veery
Towhees: rufous-sided
Vireos: red-eyed, solitary, warbling
Warblers: American redstart, ovenbird, yellow, yellowthroat (many others during migration)
Waxwings: cedar
Woodpeckers: downy, hairy, yellow-bellied sapsucker, yellow-shafted flicker
Wrens: house

The quiet of large, well-landscaped cemeteries such as Boston's Mount Auburn attracts many birds, particularly during migrations. The city dump of Manchester, New Hampshire, hosted an immature bald eagle in the summer of 1977. Shrikes and killdeer are also dump pickers (they scavenge not for the garbage but for the insects that swarm above the refuse). Harbors protect herons and gulls besides fishing fleets and tankers. And a lawyer, looking out his window in a downtown Boston skyscraper, was astonished one day to see a golden eagle floating by.

April
Arnold Arboretum

Common nighthawk

6 May to Bear Mountain

[SOUTHERN WOODLANDS]

A rufous-sided towhee trills, "Drink your tea," as we push through the bushes toward the Under Mountain Trail. This feeder trail, just north of Salisbury, Connecticut, on CT 41, climbs two miles to the famous Appalachian Trail, which we plan to follow a short distance north to the summit of Bear Mountain.

The mountain laurel bursts upon us as soon as we reach the blue-blazed trail. What a beautiful display! The chickadees and nuthatches skip through the trees. A northern oriole brightens the dark, damp woods with his lovely song. A blue jay warns all the inhabitants that we are here.

The trail climbs steeply. Wearing strong shoes or hiking boots makes sense in this terrain. Through the trees on our lower left we see sky. A palm warbler wags its tail (up and down, unlike a dog) and trots through a Christmas fern. This ground-feeding bird has a chestnut cap and yellow belly. His migration travels are taking him through these woods to his nesting site in northern Maine or Canada.

A tufted titmouse flies across an opening in a stand of birches and lights on a branch about forty feet away. We sit still, back against a young oak, and entice him by copying his "dee, dee." As tame as the chickadee, he comes closer and closer. A wave of gray wings, and he is gone: fellow hikers are coming up the path.

Two young women with large, green backpacks walk purposefully. Only when we say, "Hi," do they notice us. Through hikers, they have made distance their goal and seem to notice little of their commonplace surroundings; the glow of the laurels, the flip of a chipmunk's tail, and the gentle chip of an unseen bird go unheeded. They continue on their hurried way.

We pick ourselves up and poke along, well behind. A brown thrasher opens his bill wide and pours out a long song that almost sounds familiar. Although he imitates other birds, his song is definitely his own, as he splices his own notes between pieces of stolen tunes. A large chestnut-colored bird with a heavily streaked breast, he

Spring Birds
Bear Mountain

Chickadees: black-capped, tufted titmouse
Creeper: brown
Crows: common
Cuckoos: black-billed, yellow-billed
Falcons: American kestrel (sparrow hawk)
Finches: American goldfinch, house, pine siskin, purple
Flycatchers: eastern phoebe, eastern wood pewee, great crested, least
Gnatcatcher: blue-gray
Goatsuckers: common nighthawk, whip-poor-will
Grosbeaks: cardinal, evening, rose-breasted
Grouse: ruffed
Hawks: red-shouldered, red-tailed, sharp-shinned
Hummingbirds: ruby-throated
Jays: blue
Kingbirds: eastern
Kinglets: golden-crowned, ruby-crowned
Mimics: brown thrasher, gray catbird, mockingbird
Nuthatches: red-breasted, white-breasted

Orioles: northern (Baltimore)
Owls: barred, great horned, screech
Sparrows: dark-eyed (slate-colored) junco, fox, house, song, swamp, tree, white-crowned, white-throated
Starling: starling
Swallows: barn, tree
Tanagers: scarlet
Thrushes: American robin, hermit, Swainson's, veery, wood
Towhees: rufous-sided
Vireos: red-eyed, solitary, warbling, white-eyed, yellow-throated
Warblers: American redstart, black-and-white, blackpoll, black-throated green, blue-winged, Canada, Cape May, chestnut-sided, golden-winged, magnolia, Nashville, ovenbird, palm, pine, prairie, worm-eating, yellow, yellow-rumped, yellowthroat
Waxwings: cedar
Woodpeckers: downy, hairy, pileated, red-bellied, yellow-bellied sapsucker, yellow-shafted flicker
Wrens: Carolina, winter

should not be confused with the wood thrush. He perches in the open now but will sing from under cover while helping his mate with nesting chores.

A thin-voiced warbler song comes from nearby. We search slowly. Warblers are so hard to find. The time spent in winter in front of a roaring fire with a Cornell record of warbler songs is appreciated now. While we never see the bird whose song we hear, we know it to be a bay-breasted, black-and-white, or Cape May warbler.

The trail passes through a swamp. A silent hawk glides away. We climb again and reach the Appalachian Trail. A turn to the right starts us on the final leg to Bear Mountain. The way is well blazed, this time in white, but there are no signs. It is rocky climbing now, with the trail worn six inches deep by the thousands of hikers who have passed through.

The clouds lower. It is cool and misty. The laurels make a dripping tunnel. On the ground a worm-eating warbler runs, tail high. We think we hear a chipping sparrow's song in the moist woods, but conclude that

May
Bear Mountain

Brown thrasher

the song probably comes from the worm-eating warbler instead.

The contours of the low rock monument on the summit are softened by the swirling mists: no long views today. Moisturebeads hanging on a spider web line offer a beautiful closeup view, though.

We rest on the way down the trail, back against a smooth maple, chewing an apple. A pair of cardinals — he in his striking red feathers, she in her subtle hint of red — are working on a fallen silver birch. He hangs upside-down after some tasty morsel. Never have we seen one in this undignified position. A cardinal should be proper, not make us laugh with his antics. The pair fluff their feathers and fly, a bright finish to a gray Connecticut day.

May
Bear Mountain

7 May on the Stratford Marshes

[SOUTHERN COAST]

The Stratford marshes off CT 113 cover many acres of land between the Lordship Airport, the factories, and the barrier beach on Long Island Sound. There is no established trail, although the beach has a sandy road running through it. The marshes can best be seen by small rowboat or canoe, but rubber boots, determination, and bug spray take us through by foot this time.

The sand is strewn with shells; the Sound is strewn with sails. And on the protected side of the barrier beach, as the tide runs out, the herons appear. Far to our left a great blue heron wades through the tall rushes. Like an accountant of Dickens' time with a quill over his ear, he has a "feather in his cap" that extends beyond his head. His long legs give him a stride to match. When he spots a school of herrings he is as still as a tree on a windless day. His strong, heavy beak flashes down on his coiled-springed neck, and he catches his prey.

Here and there snowy egrets are visible. Their showy plumes ruffle in the sea breeze. Feet in the oozy muck, they busily walk about. Seven snowies in one small area! We remember a few years ago when such a sighting would have been impossible. Their territory has expanded greatly as they make their comeback from near extinction. The decorative plumes on his back were used by the ladies early in this century to decorate their backs. What a shame it would have been to lose these "dandies."

A lone cattle egret walks. This species arrived from Africa only a few short years ago and, although rare, has found a niche in America that it is beginning to fill. Its shorter, heavier bill and generally thicker appearance distinguishes it from other light herons, as does the buffy breast.

Black-crowned night herons fish in these marshes

May
Stratford Marshes

Spring Birds
Stratford Marshes

Blackbirds: brown-headed cowbird, common grackle, red-winged
Cormorants: double-crested, great
Crows: common
Doves: mourning, rock (pigeon)
Ducks: American wigeon, black, blue-winged teal, bufflehead, canvasback, common goldeneye, common merganser, common scoter, gadwall, greater scaup, green-winged teal, hooded merganser, lesser scaup, mallard, northern shoveler, oldsquaw, pintail, red-breasted merganser, ring-necked, ruddy, surf scoter, white-winged, wood
Eagles: bald (rarely)
Geese: brant, Canada, snow (blue)
Grebes: horned, pied-billed, red-necked
Gulls: Bonaparte's, great black-backed, herring, laughing, ring-billed
Hawks: marsh

Herons: American bittern, black-crowned night, cattle egret, glossy ibis, great blue, great (common) egret, green, least bittern, little blue, Louisiana, snowy egret, yellow-crowned night
Kingfishers: belted
Loons: common, red-throated
Osprey: osprey
Oystercatchers: American
Plovers: black-bellied, killdeer, piping, ruddy turnstone, semipalmated
Rails: American coot, clapper, common gallinule, sora, Virginia
Sandpipers: dunlin, greater yellowlegs, knot, least, lesser yellowlegs, pectoral, purple, sanderling, semipalmated, solitary, spotted, western, white-rumped
Sparrows: chipping, field, house, savannah, seaside, sharp-tailed, song, swamp, tree, vesper, white-throated
Starling: starling
Terns: common, least, roseate
Vultures: turkey
Wrens: long-billed marsh, short-billed marsh

33

also. For years ornithologists debated whether these night-fishing birds could see in the dark or whether they had a light. This light was supposed to issue from the chest and have the illumination of several fireflies. Herons are eye-catching enough without this imaginative addition. The young of these birds and of the yellow-crowned night heron climb from the coarse stick nests in trees to the tops of the trees to escape predators. They use their heads as a hook to help pull themselves up. When they leave the nest, the immature herons often migrate a hundred miles that same season to a different feeding ground.

Horned grebes swim in a cove. They are late migrating to their summer homes in the far northwest. Aquatic birds, they have neither the webbed feet nor the flat bills of ducks. They often sleep while floating with their heads twisted on their backs, bills tucked underwing.

May
Stratford Marshes

Least terns are busy fishing. Snow fencing has been placed around the perimeter of their nesting area. Ten pairs were discovered nesting here a few years ago. The efforts of the Connecticut Audubon Society's work force have certainly paid off: this year there are seventy pairs. High tides and rats are natural enemies to these smallest of terns' eggs. The rats are controllable; the tides are not.

Terns circle about thirty feet above the running salt water as the marsh drains. At times they hover just above the rippling water, splashing down again and again for quick shrimp meals when the tiny shellfish are caught in the shallows of the receding tide. The water boils with small fishes. We watch as a tern flips on his head and dives, folding his wings on impact. Often one will miss, but when he does get a minnow, he is in the air again almost immediately, shaking his head like a Labrador retriever.

Two black-bellied plovers race like high-stepping, well-bred trotting ponies along the mud flats toward us. The largest of the plover family to be seen in New England, they are highly visible among the "peeps" who are scouring the area for food. One drills deep with his thick bill in the muck for a marine worm. Hunger satisfied for now, he takes off across a rippling stream, the last of the tidal runoff. A clear, three-syllabled "pee-oo-wee" floats out across the marsh.

How wonderful these marshes are: so alive with birds just beyond the fringe of city life. An osprey sails in the sun, and we are blinded for the moment.

May
Stratford Marshes

Snowy egret

8 May Around the Isles of Shoals

[NORTHERN COAST/DEEP SEA]

Cut off from the world on the treeless Isles of Shoals, Celia Thaxter wrote her prose and poetry from these barren rocks off Portsmouth, New Hampshire. Birds were her beloved companions. Her bird lists are the first known for these lonely islets.

"Across the narrow beach we flit,
  one little sandpiper and I,
And fast I gather, bit by bit,
  the scattered driftwood bleached and dry.
The wild waves reach their hands for it,
  the wild wind raves, the tide runs high,
As up and down the beach we flit, —
One little sandpiper and I . . ."

You can coast the Isles of Shoals today, spend a week at a church conference on Star Island, or study marine biology through a university program. My introduction to these rocks was with the New Hampshire Audubon

Society on their annual Mother's Day visit. Although the islands are privately owned, the society has permission to come ashore and band birds.

A lovely, blustery day greets the *Viking Queen* as it sails from Portsmouth harbor past the Coast Guard station toward the Isles of Shoals, just visible ten miles away. Herring and great black-backed gulls fly overhead. Small white-capped waves pass unfelt under the bow of the boat. As we enter the protected harbor of these wind-raked islands, cormorants spread their wings out to dry on Square Rock. It is less than an hour from dock to dock. We clamber up a long ladder to the wharf (it is low tide).

The ornithologists in the group gather those of us who are beginners into the banding act. We stretch the gossamer nets between bushes and then walk toward them from a distance, driving the birds in the undergrowth before us. They tangle their feet, hanging helplessly. The gentle hands of an expert quickly disengage a female ruby-crowned kinglet. An aluminum band with an identifying number is clipped around one of her legs. She is released as another bird, a Cape May warbler, is caught.

Since 1920 these bands have helped ornithologists learn more about birds' habits and movements. They glean arrival and departure dates, how long an individual stops in migration for food and rest, how weather affects the start of a migration, if an individual returns to the same nesting site, and exact migration routes — all from the tiny leg bands. If you happen on an injured or dead bird with a band, remove, flatten, and send it along with the exact location and date to: Bird Banding Office, Patuxent Research Refuge, Fish and Wildlife Service, Laurel, Maryland 20810. The band will be returned as a souvenir if you so request.

We let the professionals continue their work. Climbing over ledges, we poke in tidal pools and watch the sandpipers. A purple sandpiper, late leaving for his northern summer grounds, combs the rockweed of a nearby pool. Our binoculars constantly sweep the swells. The small whitecaps look confusingly like gulls riding lightly. We spot a ring-billed gull and some terns.

Very few song and garden birds nest on these islets, although many migrate through. The limited land mass can only support one pair of a particular species. Since most birds seem to want more of their kind around once the breeding season is over, they don't return a second season. Loneliness is part of island living.

A toot from the boat's whistle brings us on the run. It's time to take off on the second half of this excursion, a trip to Jeffrey's Ledge. Those who expect to see a shoal awash with waves are disappointed, for this ledge is deep under water. Plankton and small marine creatures well up from the bottom, providing easy living for the deep ocean birds.

Someone yells, "gannet diving!" In the distance a large white bird with black wingtips plummets straight down, hitting the water with a splash that sprays ten feet into the air. It is said that a gannet-wise fisherman can tell the depth to set his nets for fish by the height of the gannets as they dive. A low dive means they don't have to plunge deep in the water after a fish.

Wilson's storm-petrels skip along the waves a few weeks ahead of the main flight. These martin-sized birds reverse the usual migration pattern by breeding in

Spring Birds
Isles of Shoals

Alcids: black guillemot
Blackbirds: brown-headed cowbird, common grackle, red-winged
Chickadees: black-capped
Cormorants: double-crested, great
Crows: common (rarely)
Ducks: common eider, gadwall, greater scaup (rarely), red-breasted merganser, scoters
Finches: American goldfinch
Gulls: black-legged kittiwake, Bonaparte's, great black-backed, herring, laughing, ring-billed
Herons: black-crowned night, least bittern, little blue, snowy egret
Jays: blue
Kinglets: golden-crowned, ruby-crowned

Loons: common, red-throated
Mimics: gray catbird
Osprey: osprey
Plovers: ruddy turnstone
Sandpipers: Baird's, knot, purple, sanderling, semipalmated, spotted
Sparrows: Lincoln's, savannah, song, swamp, white-crowned, white-throated
Terns: arctic, Caspian, common
Thrushes: hermit, veery, wood
Towhees: rufous-sided
Warblers: (many during migration)
Wrens: house

Deep sea birds by Jeffrey's Ledge include the gannet, Wilson's storm-petrels, northern and red phalaropes, and greater and sooty shearwaters.

the Antarctic summer and then flying seven thousand miles to the northern hemisphere's waters to summer again. On a calm day they appear to flit like bats or butterflies, but today's breezes let them set their wings.

Sailors have always feared petrels as a warning that a storm was approaching. Their superstition is based on the fact that petrels often flock around a boat looking for food just before a storm, as all birds seek food to help them through bad weather.

As a final thrill we see several northern phalaropes floating easily. Unlike most species, it is the female here that is the most colorful and who does most of the courting. Occasionally these birds are seen on New England marshes or fresh-water ponds after a driving east wind, spinning round and round, roiling the mud. They stir up plankton and tiny aquatic creatures for a seafood stew.

The long trip back to shore is filled with the excited chatter of birders who have added firsts to their life bird lists.

May
Isles of Shoals

Gannet

39

9 May in Maidstone

[NORTHERN WOODLANDS]

A dirt corduroy road only a half mile from VT 102 in Vermont's Maidstone State Park winds bumpily into the woods. Part of the Vermont trail system, it has blue blazes at regular intervals. This logging road with its varied bird habitats is perfect for searching out migrating spring warblers.

The blue spruces are heavily scented in the wet. Beneath, the bushes are alive with Nashville warblers on the move. Although first discovered near Nashville, Tennessee, this small bright bird nests in the northern woods. Its nest is seldom seen, it is so well concealed in tussocks of sphagnum moss. The young are ready to leave only eleven days after hatching, yet only one brood a year is raised. The attrition rate of warblers must be very low, since this is a most abundant family of birds.

Scattered among the flock of Nashvilles, a few Canada warblers flaunt their black pearl neckpieces. One sings from a branch in a silver birch. His song is canarylike. He is a credit to the warblers, who generally chip or buzz, not warble.

An opening ahead turns out to be a large raspberry patch that surely attracts bears come July. More warblers cross. Our binoculars are effective here, where there is time to focus them.

A male black-throated blue warbler buzzes his song from high above, while the gorgeous orange and black of a male Blackburnian warbler decorates a nearby white pine. We study the differences between a bay-breasted and a chestnut-sided warbler as one follows the other across the opening.

Around a bend in the road a small bog is alive with the peeping, quacking, croaking, and zinging of frogs. A gray jay sits atop a dead tree. The "whiskey jack," unlike other jays, is quite fearless around man. This one trails us for a handout. The familiar name probably comes from the Algonquin Indian word for him, "wis-kedjak," which means "meat bird." On a canoe trip in northern Maine one stole a piece of bacon from my frypan on the fire — hot feet! He is seldom seen south of the White Mountains.

A yellow warbler greets us at the far edge of the bog. He sits in an alder bush and burbles his beautiful song. A constant singer, he warbles, according to one estimate, 3,240 songs a day during the courting of the female! Other notes seem to be sung just for joy. Easy to see, the yellow warbler is lovely.

A brook bubbles across the road; the bumping rocks sound like a marimba. We sit and wait at this likely bird habitat. An answering bubbling is exciting. It is the winter wren. Smaller than the house wren but similar in coloring, the winter wren continually bobs his head and cocks his stubby tail as he hops on the fallen log toward cover. He is wary — hard to see. Thoreau said of his song, "It reminded me of a fine corkscrew stream, issuing with incessant lisping tinkle from a cork, flowing rapidly, and I said that he had pulled out the spile and left it running. . . . The note was so incessant that at length you only noticed when it ceased."

The road is now much narrower, less traveled, and dark under tall pines that have not been touched recently by lumbermen. This private place is the hangout of Vermont's state bird, the hermit thrush. He is the only New England thrush with a reddish brown rump and tail, which contrasts with the olive brown of the rest

41

of his upper parts. Like most other thrushes, he sports a speckled chest.

The hermit thrush has been called the American nightingale because of the genius of his song. The naturalist-painter Audubon, in one of his rare errors, stated that it had *no* song! Like the robin, another thrush, he starts his tunes an hour before sunrise, sings his hymns throughout the day, and continues after sunset. As the name implies, the hermit thrush is generally a deep woods loner, nesting on or close to the ground and raising two or three broods a year. All that glorious singing just for the jack rabbits!

Spring Birds
Maidstone Park

Blackbirds: brown-headed cowbird, common grackle, red-winged, rusty
Chickadees: black-capped, boreal
Creeper: brown
Crows: common, common raven
Cuckoos: black-billed
Doves: mourning
Ducks: black, bufflehead, common goldeneye, common merganser, green-winged teal, hooded merganser, mallard, pintail, ring-necked, wood
Eagles: bald (nesting)
Finches: American goldfinch, pine siskin, purple, red crossbill, white-winged crossbill
Flycatchers: alder (Traill's), eastern phoebe, eastern wood pewee, great crested, least, olive-sided, yellow-bellied
Geese: Canada
Goatsuckers: common nighthawk, whip-poor-will
Grebes: horned, pied-billed, red-necked
Grosbeaks: pine, rose-breasted
Grouse: ruffed, spruce
Gulls: ring-billed
Hawks: broad-winged, goshawk, red-shouldered, red-tailed, sharp-shinned
Herons: American bittern, great blue
Hummingbirds: ruby-throated
Jays: blue, gray
Kingbirds: eastern
Kingfishers: belted
Kinglets: golden-crowned, ruby-crowned
Loons: common

Mimics: brown thrasher, gray catbird
Nuthatches: red-breasted, white-breasted
Orioles: northern (Baltimore)
Owls: barred, great horned, long-eared, saw-whet, screech
Plovers: killdeer
Sandpipers: solitary, spotted
Shrikes: northern
Snipe: common
Sparrows: chipping, dark-eyed (slate-colored) junco, field, house, Lincoln's, song, swamp, tree, vesper, white-throated
Starling: starling
Swallows: barn, tree
Swifts: chimney
Tanagers: scarlet
Thrushes: American robin, gray-cheeked, hermit, Swainson's, veery, wood
Towhees: rufous-sided
Vireos: Philadelphia, red-eyed, solitary, warbling, yellow-throated
Warblers: American redstart, bay-breasted, black-and-white, Blackburnian, blackpoll, black-throated blue, black-throated green, Canada, Cape May, chestnut-sided, magnolia, mourning, Nashville, northern waterthrush, ovenbird, palm, parula, pine, prairie, Tennessee, Wilson's, yellow, yellow-rumped, yellowthroat
Waxwings: cedar
Woodcock: American
Woodpeckers: black-backed three-toed, downy, hairy, pileated, yellow-bellied sapsucker
Wrens: house, winter

As we turn to leave, a black-and-white warbler peeks around a tree stump. Similar in appearance to the striped male, this female seems to be agitated. She flutters to the ground and makes her painful way to a low shrub where she hides. Like the killdeer, she is decoying us away from her nest. We peek into the hole on the opposite side of the decaying stump to see the five creamy white eggs with their brown and lavender speckles. They should be hatching shortly. When half grown, the chicks of the black-and-white warblers readily hide on the forest floor when frightened away from their snug nest, although they are unable to fly.

After a day concentrating on warblers we understand why this season is the easiest time to identify the males. Later their bright spring plumages will molt to a more subdued "work-a-day suit." Although they keep their distinctive patterns (except for the blackpoll and bay-breasted males who at that time of year resemble their mates), it is difficult to distinguish them. All but hard-core birders have trouble identifying fall warblers!

While in the Northeast Kingdom of Vermont, we take a side trip along the dirt road that runs from Guildhall through Granby to Victory. With houses miles apart, long views and marshes to peruse, it is thirty miles of wonderful birding wilderness.

May
Maidstone

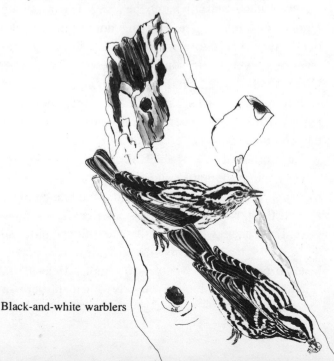

Black-and-white warblers

10 June on Quaddick Reservoir

[SOUTHERN WOODLANDS/FRESH WATER]

We heft the canoe off the car, throw our knapsacks into the middle, and slip it into the water. The launching ramp at Quaddick State Park in Thompson, Connecticut, gives access to a reservoir 1½ miles long. Immediately, we put up some black ducks. They were hiding in the cattails right by the ramp. Blacks are surface-feeding ducks. When taking off, they leap vertically out of the water while diving ducks, such as the common goldeneye, have to patter across the water's surface to gain speed before lifting into the air.

We explore the nooks and crannies of the coastline by the park. An eastern kingbird sits on a branch overlooking the expanse of the lake — a perfect fly-catching view. Dark back, white breast, a white-tipped tail, and a "square" head describe the kingbird. His orange head stripe is seldom visible, so is not a field mark. (Field marks are distinctive, quickly seen identifiers for the birder.) An aggressive bird, the male kingbird sometimes sits on the back of a crow in flight, pecking with his sharp beak at this enemy of all small songbirds.

Crossing the lake, we watch fluorescent green fish swim lazily under the canoe. Two hawks appear just over the trees from the west. The crow-sized Cooper's hawk is very similar in appearance to the smaller sharp-shinned hawk, both of whom we know inhabit this corner of Connecticut. The tip of the Cooper's tail is rounded, while that of the sharp-shinned is square. As they come within binocular's range, we identify them as Cooper's. The songbirds have all fallen silent at their approach for, as hawks often do, these two warned of their proximity by a "cuck, cuck." Swift, agile, and powerful, one plunges through a thicket, scaring birds into flight across an opening where they outmaneuver them for a successful end to their hunt.

At the far edge of the lake a low bridge forces us to duck as we pass into the reservoir's boggy end. Spotted sandpipers run along the mud flats. The spotted sandpiper, the most common and widely distributed shore bird in North America, is at home on both fresh and salt water. This "teeter-tail" shares his unique, perpetual tail-bobbing with the northern waterthrush. Within binocular range a male gives a courtship display on a rock. He puffs his feathers to make himself look big and bows with his tail toward all directions. In a few weeks the grass-lined depression in a field or near water that serves as a nest will boast the tiny spotted sandpiper young, who begin bowing almost as soon as they hatch. The spotted sandpiper can surface dive and swim underwater. We have even seen one walking on the bottom, completely submerged. The high-pitched "peet, peet" of this group follows them as they fly to the next cove.

A green heron flushes from the bushes. Long-toed footprints mark the mud beneath. As we round the next bend, we spot him waiting for us in a young oak tree. We see his crest quite plainly, although usually it is not visible. The deep warm brown, green, and blue of his feathers meld into an overall dark appearance. Green

June
Quaddick Reservoir

45

herons often nest in a white pine fifteen or twenty feet off the ground. It is a ragged nest of sticks — often the eggs show from beneath. The young climb around the tree before they can fly. Like all herons, they eat snails, leeches, frogs, insects, and fingerling fish. Although herons are often "removed" (shot) by game wardens because of their known appetite for trout, they are beneficial, even in the stocked trout ponds. They also eat many injurious insects.

We catch sight of another member of the heron family hiding in his unique style. The American bittern is frozen — neck and bill straight up. With his brown breast stripes running vertically, he imitates the marsh reeds behind him. A veritable hermit, he prefers hunching along the unwalkable edge of an oozy sinkhole to scouring the open flats like other herons.

June
Quaddick Reservoir

Late Spring Birds
Quaddick Reservoir

Blackbirds: brown-headed cowbird, common grackle, red-winged
Bluebirds: eastern
Chickadees: black-capped, tufted titmouse
Creeper: brown
Crows: common
Cuckoos: black-billed, yellow-billed
Doves: mourning
Ducks: black, common goldeneye, common merganser, mallard
Falcons: American kestrel (sparrow hawk)
Finches: American goldfinch, house
Flycatchers: alder (Traill's), eastern phoebe, eastern wood pewee, least
Gnatcatcher: blue-gray
Goatsuckers: common nighthawk, whip-poor-will
Grebes: pied-billed
Grosbeaks: cardinal
Grouse: bobwhite, ruffed
Hawks: broad-winged, Cooper's, marsh, red-shouldered, red-tailed, sharp-shinned
Herons: American bittern, black-crowned night, great blue, green
Hummingbirds: ruby-throated
Jays: blue

Kingbirds: eastern
Kingfishers: belted
Mimics: brown thrasher, gray catbird, mockingbird
Nuthatches: white-breasted
Orioles: northern (Baltimore)
Owls: barn, barred, great horned, long-eared, saw-whet, screech, short-eared
Plovers: killdeer
Rails: American coot, common gallinule, king, sora, Virginia
Sandpipers: solitary, spotted
Snipe: common
Sparrows: chipping, field, house, savannah, song
Starling: starling
Swallows: barn, tree
Swifts: chimney
Tanagers: scarlet
Thrushes: American robin, veery, wood
Towhees: rufous-sided
Vireos: red-eyed, solitary, warbling
Warblers: American redstart, black-and-white, blackpoll, blue-winged, Canada, golden-winged, ovenbird, worm-eating, yellow, yellowthroat
Waxwings: cedar
Woodcock: American
Woodpeckers: downy, hairy, yellow-bellied sapsucker, yellow-shafted flicker
Wrens: house

Often passed by when quiet, the bittern is noted for his "love song." His "oonk-ka-chunk" has been likened to the sound of an old-fashioned water pump. Forbush in his *Birds of Massachusetts* describes the method of producing the sound, " . . . a forward (horizontal) thrust of the head with opened beak whereby air was gulped — the bill being audibly snapped upon each 'mouthful.' This swallowing motion would be repeated perhaps five or six times, and during the operation a strange swelling and contortion of the neck could be plainly seen . . . There was a downward movement of the enlarged part of the neck. Then at once followed the explosive eruption of the air — the boom — closely followed by the second sound, a clear syllable 'ka'." The American bittern should attend formal dinner parties only in Arab countries where his burps would be appreciated!

We paddle back down the lake against the breeze. A kingfisher flies from tree to tree just ahead of us; a long, harsh, rattling cry streams behind him. The canoe certainly seems heavier hoisting it onto the cartop after a day's use.

June
Quaddick Reservoir

American bittern

11 June in Bear Brook

[NORTHERN WOODLANDS]

Dangling just fifteen feet above us is an oriole's nest. Bear Brook State Park's open woodlands are ideal for songbirds who are not too shy of humans, since it is a heavily used park. Located 1 mile off NH 28 between Concord and Manchester, New Hampshire, the park has thirty miles of trails along streams, up hills, through pine stands, and along tote roads. From late June until Labor Day the Audubon Center offers exhibits, field trips, evening movies, bird walks, and star-gazing walks.

We begin the ascent of Catamount Hill through a woods of young deciduous trees and older white pine. A pair of purple finches (New Hampshire's state bird) flutters through the trees. The male is rosy colored; the female looks similar to a sparrow. They drop to the ground to feed. Another male joins them, quivers his wings in an attempt to attract her, and then is driven off by the first male.

From the underbrush an ovenbird yells, "teacher

. . . Teacher . . . TEACHER!'' This common warbler with the spotted breast of a thrush is conspicuous both for its song and its lack of fear. It allows humans to approach as it scuffles in the dry leaves on the ground. Male and female are alike in dull dress, even to the Mohawk hairdo of an orange stripe from the base of the bill to the nape of the neck.

The nest of this bird is unusual. A shallow depression in the ground is roofed over and then covered with dead leaves. The opening is on the side, giving it the appearance of an old-fashioned brick oven — hence the name ovenbird.

After walking a bit over a mile, we come to Catamount Brook bubbling by mossy rocks. Bright pools of light break the dark woods. A wild honeysuckle tangles tree trunks. The sweet smell has attracted many bees and a male ruby-throated hummingbird, the only hummingbird in the East. His

---

Late Spring Birds
Bear Brook

Blackbirds: bobolink, brown-headed cowbird, common grackle, eastern meadowlark, red-winged, rusty
Bluebirds: eastern
Chickadees: black-capped
Creeper: brown
Crows: common
Cuckoos: black-billed
Doves: mourning, rock (pigeon)
Falcons: American kestrel (sparrow hawk)
Finches: American goldfinch, purple
Flycatchers: alder (Traill's), eastern phoebe, eastern wood pewee, least, olive-sided
Goatsuckers: common nighthawk, whip-poor-will
Grosbeaks: cardinal, rose-breasted
Grouse: ruffed
Hawks: broad-winged, goshawk, red-shouldered, red-tailed, sharp-shinned
Herons: American bittern, great blue
Hummingbirds: ruby-throated
Jays: blue
Kingbirds: eastern
Kingfishers: belted

Kinglets: golden-crowned, ruby-crowned
Mimics: brown thrasher, gray catbird, mockingbird
Nuthatches: red-breasted, white-breasted
Orioles: northern (Baltimore)
Owls: barred, great horned, saw-whet
Plovers: killdeer
Sandpipers: spotted
Sparrows: chipping, field, house, song, swamp, tree, white-throated
Starling: starling
Swallows: bank, barn, tree
Swifts: chimney
Tanagers: scarlet
Thrushes: American robin, hermit, Swainson's, veery, wood
Towhees: rufous-sided
Vireos: red-eyed, solitary, warbling
Vultures: turkey (rarely)
Warblers: American redstart, black-and-white, ovenbird, pine, yellow, yellow-rumped, yellowthroat
Waxwings: cedar
Woodcock: American
Woodpeckers: downy, hairy, yellow-bellied sapsucker, yellow-shafted flicker
Wrens: house

June
Bear Brook

iridescent colors shimmer in a spotlight of sun. This iridescence is caused by a refraction of light on the unique structure of the feathers. The wings whirr faster than the human eye can see. The placement of these wings is such that hummingbirds can hover as they plunge their long bills deep into the throat of a flower. Like bees, they help pollinate flowers with this action. Hummingbirds are not only nectar sippers; they also devour countless insects. The metabolism of these birds is so high that they must eat constantly.

The female hummingbird does not have the ruby throat. Her tail is rounded, while his is forked. We look in the bushes, without success, for the well-hidden, walnut-sized nest covered with lichens. Cup-shaped, it is made of plant down stuck together with stolen tent caterpillar web or spider web and custom fitted to her body. The young must develop three weeks before leaving the nest. The joy of seeing one bathe in a dewdrop, preening itself afterwards, is impossible to put into words.

After this leisurely walk around Catamount Trail, we again notice the oriole's wondrous bag of woven fibers. Having found some blown apart by winter storms, we know that the inside is lined with moss, hair, or plant fluff. In my neighborhood orioles weave their nests from all the loose white or gray strings the wind shakes free from laundry hanging on the clotheslines. Apparently, they choose these colors because they are close to the colors of natural materials. Many backyard birders deliberately hang yarn and string around their bushes to provide nesting materials for their bird neighbors.

The female of this species builds the nest. After draping a few long fibers of last year's dried weed stalks from the branches that will support it, she weaves them together. The process takes two or three days. The male, constantly whistling a gay tune, gives glorious moral support to his mate while she works. His bright colors glow against the spring green of the elm.

Oriole parents start their brood off early on hairy caterpillars — a boon to the orchardist and an important source of protein for the baby birds. The foods that have less protein come later. If a tragedy places an orphan bird in your care, check with an expert about feeding it, as birds' nutritional requirements differ. Most orphaned or injured birds, however, die from exposure if they aren't found almost immediately or from shock if they are handled too much. Young orioles seem to make it through this situation better than most other birds. The Audubon Center here in Bear Brook skillfully handles many injured birds each summer.

As we leave the park, the sight of four huge birds slowly circling overhead makes us pull up quickly. We are dumbfounded to see turkey vultures in New Hampshire. Like many birds, they are moving north into New England. While species such as the mockingbird and cardinal seem to be appearing because developments are encroaching on their more usual southern territories, the turkey vulture seems to be a victim of high-speed, heavy traffic and needs the slower pace of these parts to survive. These four hardly flap their wings as they easily rise on a thermal from the heat of the pavement.

June
Bear Brook

Ruby-throated hummingbirds

12 June on the Moriah Trail

[NORTHERN WOODLANDS]

Just north of Evans Notch on ME 113 a well-maintained dirt road takes us across the state line to the primitive campground on New Hampshire's Wild River. The Moriah Trail, a north-woods path where understory birds such as warblers and thrushes abound, begins on the far side of the river.

We cross the sturdy wooden bridge, thankful that the original cables we once inched across have been replaced. Tiny tree swallows swoop beneath the bridge, skimming the water's surface after insects. They appear in northern New England earlier in the year than other swallows, since they can subsist on berries that have survived the winter. We spot their neat nests tucked in crevices along the bridge supports, and we wonder where so deep in the woods they found the white feathers that line them. They normally use chicken feathers found in farmyards, yet the nearest farm is ten miles over the mountains.

We notice five young tree swallows sitting in a row

on a leafless limb. Adults are feeding them. Later they will be fed on the wing to supplement their own meagre catches until they are capable of sustaining themselves completely. The five young launch themselves. As they arc through the air, we think that their glowing, graceful bodies should house a lilting song, instead of the "scritch" they do.

Following the north bank of Wild River, the Moriah Trail wanders through a hemlock stand on a bluff rising from the water's edge. Silver flashes reflecting off the rippling waters below make a light show on the dense branches above our heads. We catch glimpses of chickadees and nuthatches as we walk carefully on the slippery, dry hemlock needles.

Through a break in the trees we spot a male belted kingfisher perched on a branch overhanging the river. He dives, and a minnow shines from his heavy beak. Flying directly to the bluff, he disappears into a nesting hole. Both bank swallows and kingfishers use the same size hole, often in the same bank. We look for the set of "ski tracks" on the bottom lip of his hole. When the kingfisher flies from its hole, it drags its feet; the swallow lifts more quickly, leaving a flat, unmarked lip. His mate flies from the hole. Unlike most birds, the female kingfisher is "fancier dressed" than the male. She has an extra belt of rust crossing her chest.

After one-half mile the trail branches to the right to follow Moriah Brook. Red crossbills feed on the cones of a spruce. We watch one of these brick red birds use its strange bill to pull the scales from a cone, unveiling the seeds. We lie on the cool ground for a good view. Like the parrot at the pet store, the crossbill also uses its bill to help climb through the twigs. Unsuspicious, handsome, acrobatic — that's the crossbill.

Moriah Brook is lost to the left as the widened trail passes through a mixed second-growth forest. The White Mountain National Forest, through which this path wanders, is used not only for recreation but also for logging. The cutover areas produce berry bushes and meadow grasses that make extra feed for both birds and mammals.

June
Moriah Trail

A brooklet trickles across the trail on its way to the Androscoggin River: clear, clean, cold, and delicious. We try to clamber over the rocks quietly, slowly, as a magnolia warbler splashes in a tiny pool. Flitting nervously, it darts away. Probably hidden in the undergrowth nearby is its abandoned nest of spider webs and dried cinquefoils. The young have already "flown the coop."

Returning to the path, we continue toward Moriah Gorge. Far below on our left, the brook appears again. Sliding down the wall of the gorge, a steep, tree-covered embankment, we know it's going to be a tree-to-tree climb back up.

Room-sized boulders piled on top of each other block the brook, making ten-foot-deep pools. So clear is the water that the pools look only three feet deep. Trout wave their tails. The roar of waterfalls upstream draws us higher. The way is blocked by an overhanging cliff so we remove our shoes and plunge into the icy water. The sight is worth the gasp! A series of waterfalls

Early Summer Birds
Moriah Trail

Chickadees: black-capped, boreal
Creeper: brown
Crows: common, common raven
Cuckoos: black-billed
Eagles: bald, golden (both rarely)
Falcons: peregrine (rarely)
Finches: American goldfinch, pine siskin, purple, red crossbill, white-winged crossbill
Flycatchers: alder (Traill's), eastern wood pewee, great crested, olive-sided, yellow-bellied
Goatsuckers: common nighthawk, whip-poor-will
Grosbeaks: rose-breasted
Grouse: ruffed, spruce
Hawks: broad-winged, goshawk, red-tailed
Herons: great blue
Hummingbirds: ruby-throated
Jays: blue, gray (rarely)
Kingbirds: eastern
Kingfishers: belted
Kinglets: golden-crowned, ruby-crowned
Mimics: brown thrasher, gray catbird

Nuthatches: red-breasted, white-breasted
Orioles: northern (Baltimore)
Owls: barred, great horned, saw-whet
Sandpipers: spotted
Sparrows: swamp, white-throated
Starling: starling
Swallows: bank, tree
Tanagers: scarlet
Thrushes: American robin, hermit, Swainson's, veery, wood
Towhees: rufous-sided
Vireos: Philadelphia, red-eyed, solitary
Warblers: American redstart, bay-breasted, black-and-white, Blackburnian, blackpoll, black-throated blue, black-throated green, Canada, chestnut-sided, magnolia, mourning, Nashville, ovenbird, parula, yellow, yellow-rumped, yellowthroat
Waxwings: cedar
Woodcock: American
Woodpeckers: black-backed three-toed, downy, hairy, pileated, yellow-bellied sapsucker, yellow-shafted flicker
Wrens: house, winter

feed a small, hidden basin. The masked intruder, a yellowthroat, inquires, "whatcha see, whatcha see," and then impatiently darts to another shrub, chattering all the while. This bright, highly visible warbler is beloved by birders for his wrenlike behavior. When he is suddenly gone, we are utterly alone.

The climb back out of the gorge is steep and hard, and the feel of individual trees is alternately smooth and rough to our hands. The hundreds of holes, row upon row, in a birch tree can only mean a yellow-bellied sapsucker has been busy on this slope. Yellow-bellied sapsucker — the name that brings laughter to so many people. After the bird drills the holes, he returns for the sap that fills them. He is industrious and retiring and does not deserve that laughter.

We return on the easy, downhill path to Wild River. A few years ago a friend and I stepped out of the brush here to pick raspberries along the bank. If we hadn't reached the open at just that moment, we never would have noticed a distant light speck high above. As it

June
Moriah Trail

Kingfisher

swept swiftly down the river course and became more distinct, we recognized a peregrine falcon! A visitor from the far north, he is seldom seen this side of the Canadian border. All the Persian miniatures picturing the magnificent falcon on a nobleman's wrist can never replace that instant of time for me. He was gone before our hearts started beating again.

Naturally, the bird blown off course in a storm or the extremely rare visitor should not be expected on any field trip. But being alert for any occurrence, at any time, makes being within nature exciting.

June
Moriah Trail

13 July in a Farm Field

[FIELDS]

Wrens burble their songs from the fence post, meadowlarks and bobolinks flit through the tall grass, sparrows and robins follow the tractor, and swallows flip and dip overhead. Birds find farm fields an attractive habitat. From northern Maine to southern Connecticut we find many of the same species feeding on their lush grains and plentiful insects. A farmer whose fields we are admiring invites us to go birding through his stone wall-rimmed territory, reminding us to shut all gates and watch where we step.

On a pole above the farmyard perches a small penthouse. Obviously this farmer knows the value of birds. Swallows and purple martins fly in clouds around the nearby fields, the garden, and in the dooryard, keeping the mosquito population down. Within view of the kitchen window a box sits high on a pole. A bluebird peeks out. Bluebirds are not as common as they once were, which makes them even more beloved. This flashing blue resident is not as gentle as he looks. In his book *Birds of Massachusetts and other New England States* Forbush recounts the story of a cat chased by two dogs to the top of a bluebird box. The male bluebird attacked the cat so viciously that it returned to the ground, preferring to face the dogs.

A phoebe's nest nestles in the eaves of a chick-encoop. Within, we see two small white eggs and one large speckled egg, which does not belong with the others. After waiting for the phoebe to leave, a brown-headed cowbird surreptitiously laid her egg alongside the two smaller ones, leaving it for the foster parent to hatch and raise. At times a cowbird egg is found smashed beneath another bird's nest, showing that it has not been accepted, but most often it is hatched. The hatchling is usually larger than the other chicks in the nest and therefore demands and gets most of the food, in effect killing off its assumed brothers and sisters. Because of this practice the cowbird's survival rate is high. We nonetheless resist the temptation to remove the egg.

We walk by the garden. The peas are heavy in the pod; the vines bend to the ground. The farmer had hand-cultivated this patch. "Why?" we ask ourselves. A killdeer "nest" hides between the rows; four perfectly camouflaged eggs lie directly on the ground. A killdeer female, wing dragging on the ground, screams only five feet away from us. Obviously she is in trouble. Bending over the eggs, we notice that one is

July
Farm Field

Summer Birds
Farm Field

Blackbirds: bobolink, brown-headed cowbird, common grackle, eastern meadowlark, red-winged
Bluebirds: eastern
Buntings: indigo
Chickadees: black-capped
Crows: common
Doves: mourning, rock (pigeon)
Falcons: American kestrel (sparrow hawk)
Finches: American goldfinch, dickcissel (southern New England, rarely)

Flycatchers: eastern phoebe, least (orchard), willow
Goatsuckers: common nighthawk
Grosbeaks: cardinal (hedgerow except northern New England), rose-breasted (orchard)
Grouse: bobwhite (southern New England), ruffed (orchard)
Gulls: herring, ring-billed
Hawks: Cooper's, marsh, red-shouldered, red-tailed, sharp-shinned (woods margin)
Herons: American bittern, cattle egret, great blue (all wet lowlands), green

cracked. A chick is working from within. The female flutters and falls again to the ground. She tries to draw us away from her nest with her famous broken-wing act. When we walk away, she hurries back to the eggs.

A ring-necked pheasant runs through the rows of corn as we push toward the pasture. Released from a state game farm where he has been hatched and raised, he was placed in this field for the summer. Come fall, he will be hunted for game. A magnificent tail trails behind this now-strutting male.

On turf kicked up by a high-spirited foal a male red-winged blackbird displays his epaulets to his lady-love. Only in her face-to-face position can the scarlet and yellow brilliance against his black back be truly appreciated. He hops toward her with head down and shoulders hunched. Her interest is short-lived, and they fly to a blueberry bush where he takes up a defensive watch.

A bobolink swings atop a slender weed. His bubbly song is as interesting as his coloring. A yellow cap with matching stripes down his back and a white cape draped over his black back decorate this field singer whose song cannot be imitated even by the talented mockingbird. June and early July are the times to observe the bobolinks, for soon they will be gathering for their long migration. Because bobolinks used to eat prodigious amounts of rice, ruining whole fields in the deep south, they were shot in quantity and sold at the

July
Farm Field

Hummingbirds: ruby-throated
Jays: blue
Kingbirds: eastern
Kingfishers: belted (streams)
Lark: horned
Mimics: brown thrasher, gray catbird, mockingbird
Nuthatches: white-breasted
Orioles: northern (Baltimore), orchard (southern New England)
Owls: barn, great horned, screech
Pheasant: ring-necked (except high northern New England)
Plovers: killdeer
Sandpipers: spotted

Sparrows: chipping, field, grasshopper (southern New England), house, savannah, song, tree, vesper
Starling: starling
Swallows: bank (gravel pits), barn, rough-winged (streams), purple martin
Swifts: chimney
Thrushes: American robin, wood
Towhees: rufous-sided
Waxwings: cedar
Woodcock: American (lowlands)
Woodpeckers: downy, yellow-bellied sapsucker (orchards), yellow-shafted flicker
Wrens: house

market. Few people at that time realized these "rice birds" in their dull traveling feathers were the colorful bobolinks seen in the spring. Nowadays they fly freely toward their goal in eastern South America. Their route takes them through Cuba and Jamaica, and then, braving a five-hundred-mile ocean hop, they cross the open Gulf of Mexico to the southern continent. They spend much more time in their winter home than in our farm fields.

Hidden in the deep grasses the meadowlark sings. Often the only view we get is of one fluttering five feet above the grass tips as it grabs a flying beetle.

We circle back toward the barn along the bushy hedgerow the farmer planted to break the cold northwest winds. Birds "chit" and twitter near the ground. We notice a few nests tucked deep in the brush. A catbird bounces on a thin branch, his "gray flannel suit" contrasting with his fierce, flashing eyes. He disappears through the trees as a large yellow tomcat rounds the corner of the barn, his tail twitching ever so slightly. He pounces, and a mouse scurries across the yard. His disappointed meow is echoed by the now-distant catbird.

July
Farm Field

Killdeer

14 July on the *Bluenose*

[NORTHERN COAST/DEEP SEA]

The uninhabited, spruce-tipped, granite chunk islets off the coast of Maine attract innumerable birds to their private worlds. The abstract swirling patterns of fog often hide the swooping gulls. Beard moss, the home of parula warblers, hangs heavy. Island-hopping is a joy. As we travel north along the coast toward our rendezvous with the ferry *Bluenose,* which will take us to Nova Scotia, we watch these islands slip past like so many tall ships at sea.

Matinicus Rock, the most southerly nesting area for common puffins, protects a few nesting pairs. Although we have a reservation on the mail boat to Matinicus, fierce weather and then an engine failure cancel our plans. The only other place to find puffins on the U.S. Atlantic coast is at Machias Seal Island. My first acquaintance with these "parrots of the ocean" was at Percé Rock on the Gaspé Peninsula in Canada. There, hundreds of nesting puffins fall off the cliff to

61

bullet their way to the water for fish; wings whir rapidly. Since the legs of these birds are attached to the rear of their bodies, they stand upright, strong webbed feet gripping the slippery rocks, before launching themselves.

Puffins nest late in June and July. Unlike many deep sea birds, the female does not lay her eggs in a protected place on the ground but in deep burrows that the male digs with his curved, sharp claws. The claws are also strong protection in that burrow. The puffin's ludicrous bill is, and is meant to be, eye-catching; the orange horny plates are spring breeding ornaments.

We drive onto the most famous of Maine's islands, Mount Desert. The home of Acadia National Park, this island is a must for New England walkers. Bridle paths cut through northern bird habitats, and cliff-hanging paths are awesome. Bare and breezy, the top of Cadillac Mountain boasts a view of Bear, Squid, Moose, Swan, and Bald Porcupine — all islands. Night, with its moon lantern reflected in a peaceful sea, finds us at one of the many island campgrounds. We cook a fresh lobster in sea water, eat it, and then fall asleep to the clang of a buoy rocking in the waves.

July
the *Bluenose*

Early next morning we wait in line for the six-hour cruise from Bar Harbor to Yarmouth, Nova Scotia, aboard the *Bluenose*. As we had hoped when we made the required reservations weeks ago, the day is glorious. After parking in the amazingly large hold, we grab our heavy sweaters and binoculars and climb the stairs to the deck.

Before we even leave the dock, we catch sight of black guillemots. Since they raise their young in inaccessible rock caves, their numbers have not been as reduced as those of other sea birds whose nests are more easily reached by the "egg hunters" — not the herring gulls but people.

An immature double-crested cormorant with a bright red orange bill and pouch and steel gray feathers outlined in chocolate brown eyes us from a piling. As a passenger approaches the gangplank, the cormorant's neck stretches long, and he prepares for flight. With a short hop he settles into the water, and settles, and settles. When he swims, about all we see is his neck and head; his body is hidden beneath the surface like the famous "snake bird" of the Everglades, the anhinga. The cormorant uses both his webbed feet and his wings to propel himself through the water. Still beneath the water's surface, he "flies" by the boat, catching fish fry as he glides.

The ship's horn blasts, a shiver runs through the deck, and the voyage is underway amidst the screams of gulls, the ever-present scavengers of the sea. We leave land behind.

Greater shearwaters fly near a fishing boat on the horizon. These so-called "hags" enjoy the leftovers, as do the gulls. They nest in the South Atlantic islands and are seldom near land here on their summer vacation. A dark sooty shearwater flies with the more numerous greater shearwaters. Although common on the California coast, they are rare here. Since shearwaters are usually at a distance from the boat and fly low to the water, we find it hard to distinguish the different types.

We also spot jaegers off in the distance. Often mistaken for gulls or terns, these deep-sea birds have elongated central tail feathers and wings that are held bent like a falcon. They have another characteristic of the falcon, too, that of preying on small birds or chasing one until it drops the food it is carrying.

Closing in on Yarmouth, we are lucky enough to see a skua silhouetted against the sky. Hooked beak, fierce temperament, and solitary living have caused it to be nicknamed the sea-hawk. On these fishing banks one often pounces on refuse from the fishing boats.

Summer Birds
Bluenose

Alcids: black guillemot, common murre, common puffin, razorbill, thick-billed murre
Cormorants: double-crested, great
Ducks: black, common eider, oldsquaw, scoters
Gannet: gannet

Gulls: Arctic, Bonaparte's, great black-backed, herring, ring-billed
Jaegers: long-tailed, parasitic, pomarine (rarely)
Loons: common
Phalaropes: northern, red
Shearwaters: greater, manx, sooty
Skua: skua
Storm-Petrels: Leach's, Wilson's
Terns: Caspian, common, roseate

63

Nova Scotia hills rise from the Bay of Fundy. It's time to return to the car. A circuit of this province is bound to bring more bird sightings, as well as a dinner of scallops, sea-run trout, or fresh salmon steak.

Common puffins

July
the *Bluenose*

15 July on the Concord River

[SOUTHERN WOODLANDS/FRESH WATER]

Great Meadows National Wildlife Preserve encompasses twelve miles of the Concord River in Massachusetts. We paddle the canoe under the famous Old North Bridge, feeding the ducks that follow unhesitatingly. The Minuteman stands firmly in his statuesque stance, a pigeon ensconced on his rifle.

Concord's natural world has figured as prominently in the writings of literary giants as has its role in the Revolutionary War. Thoreau's observations are well known, but it is William Brewster's diary we recall when we find a grebe's nest hidden in some grasses near the bank of the river: "May 5, 1900: The grebe's nest was built in the center of a small cluster of leafless button bushes and was floating on water two feet deep....The grebes called every little while, at first some distance away, gradually working nearer until they were within 25 or 30 yards. They gave the cuckoo call only. We did not see either of them."

The pied-billed grebe's large nest is no stranger to

New England marshes. When she leaves her nest, she covers her eggs with mud and grasses. The nest then appears to be grassy flotsam caught in the bushes. We watch as she rides buoyantly on the water. A plane flies low, frightening her, and she dives. Grebes are known for their disappearing act. They swim long distances underwater and will remain submerged, except for their beaks and eyes, in a reedy hiding place until danger is past.

After paddling part of the upper preserve, we decide to walk the dike trail just off MA 62. History surrounds us here, for this is the same route that the British soldiers marched from Lexington to Concord. The short trail across the dikes that prevent two small duck ponds from joining the Concord River cuts through the area of Thoreau's notes on Great Meadow. Many of the same types of ducks, geese, grebes, and herons populate these marshes now as then, although we do a double-take when a great egret stalks into view around a corner. It has extended its territory north since Thoreau's time.

Solitary sandpipers pick at invisible food on the mud margin. One takes a drink, pointing its bill upward to let the water run down its throat. The ornithologist Forbush describes how these birds stir the silt without muddying the water and then catch the insect food that

Summer Birds
Concord River

Blackbirds: bobolink, brown-headed cowbird, common grackle, eastern meadowlark, red-winged
Bluebirds: eastern
Buntings: indigo
Chickadees: black-capped, tufted titmouse
Creeper: brown
Crows: common
Cuckoos: black-billed
Doves: mourning, rock (pigeon)
Ducks: black, blue-winged teal, hooded merganser, mallard, wood

Falcons: American kestrel (sparrow hawk)
Finches: dickcissel, American goldfinch, purple
Flycatchers: eastern phoebe, eastern wood pewee, great crested, willow
Geese: Canada
Grebes: pied-billed
Grosbeaks: cardinal, rose-breasted
Grouse: bobwhite, ruffed
Gulls: herring
Hawks: broad-winged, marsh, red-shouldered, red-tailed, sharp-shinned
Herons: American bittern, black-crowned night, great (common) egret, great blue, green, little blue, snowy egret
Hummingbirds: ruby-throated

has been uncovered. Dark wings extend and touch at the tips as another lands like an angel from above.

We walk past the ponds toward the river. Cedar waxwings are busy in the trees. These birds turn from insect eaters to gluttonous cherry pickers as soon as the berries set. They have also been known to become intoxicated from eating overripe chokecherries that have naturally fermented.

Black mask, a sleek brown top coat with red "sealing wax" dabs on its wings, and a yellow decorative tail band make the cedar waxwing an elegant-looking bird. Raccoons are the rascals, not the clean-cut cedar waxwing, even if the two do wear the same mask! A late nester, often raising two broods, the cedar waxwing is an attentive parent. Occasionally the second clutch of eggs is laid in the nest while the fledglings of the first brood are about ready to fly.

A beautiful tune ripples across the river. In May 1855 Thoreau's quick notes gave his impression of the same song: "Hear a rose-breasted grosbeak. At first thought it a tanager, but soon perceived its more clear and instrumental (song) — should say whistle, if one could whistle like a flute . . ."

The grosbeak takes up his song again, and now we see the crisp black and white of his back as he moves from tree to tree. As the sun hits his strawberry "birth-

July
Concord River

Jays: blue
Kingbirds: eastern
Kingfishers: belted
Mimics: brown thrasher, gray
    catbird, mockingbird
Nuthatches: white-breasted
Orioles: northern (Baltimore),
    orchard
Osprey: osprey
Owls: barred, great horned,
    long-eared, saw-whet (rarely),
    screech
Plovers: killdeer
Rails: American coot, common
    gallinule, king, sora, Virginia
Sandpipers: solitary, spotted
Snipe: common
Sparrows: chipping, field, house,
    savannah, sharp-tailed, song,
    swamp, vesper

Starling: starling
Swallows: bank, barn, cliff, tree
Swifts: chimney
Tanagers: scarlet
Thrushes: American robin, hermit,
    veery, wood
Towhees: rufous-sided
Vireos: red-eyed, solitary,
    warbling, yellow-throated
Warblers: American redstart,
    black-and-white, Nashville,
    ovenbird, parula, pine, prairie,
    yellow, yellowthroat
Waxwings: cedar
Woodcock: American
Woodpeckers: downy, hairy,
    red-headed (rarely),
    yellow-bellied sapsucker,
    yellow-shafted flicker

67

mark," it glows. The female's dull mottled appearance can be mistaken for a female purple finch's, although she is almost two inches longer. Rose-breasted grosbeaks are much more common now than in Thoreau's time. He spent years birding before the sweetness of their song attracted him. What a welcome pair to see, unlike the proliferating starlings overhead. It is incomprehensible that the one hundred starlings introduced to Central Park in 1890 could have multiplied to the ever-present flocks of today.

Canada geese nest around the edges of the ponds here in Great Meadows. From a photo-blind we watch a family of six following each other through the shallow water. An unseen flock talks from somewhere in the grasses. Suddenly it is in the air just over our heads, the birds' muscles rippling rhythmically. Like the Hobbit, or tiny Tom Thumb, we'd enjoy being lofted through the air on the back of a powerful bird.

Cedar waxwings

July
Concord River

16 July in Baxter Park

[NORTHERN WOODLANDS/FRESH WATER/
TIMBERLINE]

Nearly one hundred and fifty miles of trails wind through some two hundred *thousand* acres of wilderness in Northern Maine's Baxter Park. Some are easy walks to lovely waterfalls where the musical trill of a veery blends with the heavier beat of roaring water. Other trails are deep-knee exercises up rocky slopes to bare summits.

We pass through the gate, then enter the burned-over area that 1977's huge forest fire damaged. Black stumps with roots exposed by the plowing of bulldozers' blades for a firebreak lie every which way. Our first reaction is one of horror, but then nature's cycle becomes clear to us. At the fringe of the blackened woods, birds twitter as they flit through raspberry and blueberry bushes. Grasses are reseeding the forlorn area, attracting sparrows. Deciduous trees have a chance to grow. Instead of the mature coniferous forest that is a limited

69

habitat, we see an open habitat for myriad birds and animals.

We pass a marshy-edged pond. A moose in velvet stands in the water with a mouthful of lilies. A pair of plain brown ducks — gadwalls — dive and dive. We watch for fifteen minutes enjoying their grace. By a second small pond we stop to watch the loons parade. With binoculars we can barely make out a chick on mother's back.

After registering with a ranger, we start up Mount Katahdin by way of the Abol Trail, the oldest trail to the top. Meeting the Appalachian Trail only 2.7 miles from the Abol Campground, then finishing the climb with that illustrious trail, Abol seems a good choice. At the bottom we follow a stream and then veer through a small swamp. Fresh moose droppings show we are not the first on the trail this morning. A cardinal flower is strikingly red at pathside, the echo of a hairy wood-pecker's head patch.

We come to the bottom of the rock slide and re-member, too late, that this is the hardest way to the top of the mountain. We sit for a minute gazing in disbelief up that slide (we are two tenderfeet). Thoreau Springs on the tableland is a long mile and a half away!

The warblers that were migrating through Connec-ticut in April and southern New Hampshire in May have

July
Baxter Park

Summer Birds
Baxter Park

Blackbirds: brown-headed cowbird, common grackle, red-winged, rusty
Chickadees: black-capped, boreal
Creeper: brown
Crows: common, common raven
Cuckoos: black-billed
Doves: mourning
Ducks: black, common goldeneye, common merganser, gadwall, mallard, wood
Eagles: bald, golden
Falcons: American kestrel (sparrow hawk)
Finches: American goldfinch, pine siskin, purple, red crossbill, white-winged crossbill

Flycatchers: alder (Traill's), eastern phoebe, eastern wood pewee, least, yellow-bellied
Goatsuckers: common nighthawk, whip-poor-will
Grosbeaks: evening, pine, rose-breasted
Grouse: ruffed, spruce
Gulls: herring
Hawks: broad-winged, goshawk, red-shouldered, sharp-shinned
Herons: American bittern, great blue
Hummingbirds: ruby-throated
Jays: blue, gray
Kingbirds: eastern
Kingfishers: belted
Kinglets: golden-crowned, ruby-crowned
Loons: common

all arrived here it seems. The woods are flickering with them. They dart into the sunshine of the slide. A Blackburnian perches on the branch of an ash and watches us. His yellow-orange head and front seem to burn (as his name indicates) in the early light. His mate "chips" and off he flies. A blackpoll warbler alights briefly in a hemlock. Myrtles flit. A mourning warbler belies its name and sings joyfully.

A screaming "keow" captures our full attention. It rushes down the mountain. Only an eagle could make such a sound. No longer do Connecticut, Rhode Island, or Massachusetts have nesting eagles, but they do nest *here*. Raising only one brood of one to four chicks a year, they are barely holding their own south of Alaska. Like the osprey, many of the eagles' eggs have been made infertile by pesticide residue. The eagle has swooped down a ravine paralleling the rock slide we are continuing to struggle up.

Two young men wave to us and stop to chat on their way down the mountain. Not birders, they didn't notice the pipits which nest in the tundra area of the mountaintop. We usually see them as they alight on a plowed field during the fall migration. Plain birds, they don't hold our attention like the eye-catching Blackburnian warbler.

Although there is no vegetation in the center of the

July
Baxter Park

Mimics: gray catbird, mockingbird
Nuthatches: red-breasted,
  white-breasted
Orioles: northern (Baltimore)
Osprey: osprey
Owls: barred, great horned,
  saw-whet
Pipits: water
Plovers: killdeer
Sandpipers: solitary, spotted
Shrikes: northern
Snipe: common
Sparrows: chipping, dark-eyed
  (slate-colored) junco, Lincoln's,
  song, white-throated
Swallows: bank, barn, tree
Tanagers: scarlet
Terns: common
Thrushes: American robin, hermit,
  veery, wood

Vireos: red-eyed
Waxwings: cedar
Warblers: American redstart,
  bay-breasted, black-and-white,
  Blackburnian, blackpoll,
  black-throated blue,
  black-throated green, Canada,
  Cape May, chestnut-sided,
  magnolia, mourning, Nashville,
  northern waterthrush, ovenbird,
  palm, parula, Tennessee,
  Wilson's, yellow,
  yellow-rumped, yellowthroat
Woodcock: American
Woodpeckers: black-backed
  three-toed, downy, hairy,
  pileated, yellow-bellied
  sapsucker, yellow-shafted flicker
Wrens: house, winter

71

slide, grasses and small wild flowers decorate the edges. The spruces and birches at our side become head high, then waist high, as we near the timberline. The wind has twisted them into grotesque shapes. Only the leaves gentle their contours. The views are spectacular on this trail, since the slide has opened the sky to us. Ponds, lakes, and the distant Penobscot River glitter between stretches of fir forest. Few birds venture this high; there is little food or cover for them.

A raven with wings wide coasts on a current of air like a hawk. A large copy of the crow, its black wings spread wider than four feet, the raven squawks. The Edgar Allan Poe poem runs through my mind. The doorframe that holds a bust of Pallas *and* a raven is certainly large!

The evil portent of that raven's squawk comes true as a cloud plumps down on the mountain, shutting off our views. A few drops of rain warn us to turn back. Before we arrive at the bottom of the slide, the downpour hits.

Common raven

July
Baxter Park

The rocks are extremely slippery, and it has turned cold.

A half hour brings us to a large raspberry patch dripping in the rain. A grunting ''snorf'' warns us that a bear, unbothered by the wet, is eating. Park rules forbid feeding bears. We chuckle a bit hysterically as we hurry by.

July
Baxter Park

17 August in Norman Sanctuary

[SOUTHERN WOODLANDS/FRESH WATER/SOUTHERN COAST]

Fifteen miles of trails wander past salt, fresh, and brackish marshes, through fields, through woods in different stages of growth, up ridges of "puddingstone" and lava, and along a dune-edged beach. The number of birds which can be seen and *studied* at Norman Sanctuary is phenomenal. "New England's Largest Living Classroom" is located on Third Beach Road in Middletown, Rhode Island, just east of Newport. The sanctuary, open to the general public every afternoon, teaches ecology to thousands of children each year through its summer day camp, television program, and school programs. It also provides care and a temporary home for birds and animals who are accident victims.

After passing through a hall of exhibitions that includes a rare example of the Eskimo curlew (last seen a few years ago in Baja, Mexico, and probably extinct by now), we enter a courtyard where we are greeted by a pleasant "hello." A large crow has learned its lesson well.

A red-tailed hawk sits tethered to a perch, the victim of a modern day "falconer" who stole him as a fledgling from the nest. His release will come as soon as legalities are over, for unlicensed falconry, along with shooting hawks and eagles, is against the law. A great horned owl, blind in one eye, tries to attack us but is brought up short by the thongs tied around his legs. An injured raccoon works at the lock of its cage. And a mute swan bellies across the courtyard, barely able to hold its head up on its graceful neck. After being hit by a car and brought here for expert care, the swan is making a remarkable recovery from much brain damage.

We start down the Quarry Trail, passing several explanatory signs. These signs may tell of the cycle of a field being reclaimed by nature, a bird fact, or of an alfalfa field which has been cultivated continuously for three hundred years and is a favorite for the plovers. Great flocks of migrating plovers light in this feeding place for a respite.

Off to the right through a heavy screen of juniper, bittersweet, and cat briar a tall pole with a wagonwheel atop waits in a protected opening for an osprey to build a nest. Years ago ospreys regularly nested on this shoreline. The use of DDT in this heavily populated area contaminated the fish that are the staple in their diet, and they were unable to raise young. (The eggshells of birds that have ingested DDT are soft and may break before the young hatch.) Now that this substance has been taken off the market (except for strictly regulated uses), the osprey is making a successful comeback.

The quarry drops off suddenly on our left. Once the source of the slate that covers many mansion roofs in nearby Newport, it is now a marsh where both short-billed and long-billed marsh wrens spend their summers. Because the short-billed is an extremely shy bird, it is hard to study. A plain, small bird with a song to match, it is most often seen when flushed from the sedges.

The long-billed is definitely the more interesting "kissing cousin." Almost as large as the house wren, he sports a bright white eye stripe and a dark "cape" with white stripes. Like all wrens, he often burbles a song with his tail held straight up. The ornithologist Wilson likens his song to "air bubbles forcing their way through mud or boggy ground when trodden upon ...": not exactly beautiful, but interesting. Perpetually in motion, the male expends much of his energy building nests. They are grassy balls lined with down from nearby ducks, with a hole in the side for an entrance. Many are built, possibly as decoys.

We follow the trail to Hanging Rock, a ridge of lava covered with a conglomerate rock that looks like cobblestones. Warblers rustle through low bushes. Wide views down both sides of the bluff provide opportunities to see hawks, owls, high-flying gulls of

August
Norman Sanctuary

Summer Birds

Norman Sanctuary

Blackbirds: bobolink, brown-headed cowbird, common grackle, eastern meadowlark, red-winged
Bluebirds: eastern
Buntings: indigo
Chickadees: black-capped, tufted titmouse
Cormorants: double-crested
Crows: common, fish
Cuckoos: black-billed, yellow-billed
Doves: mourning
Ducks: American wigeon, black, mallard, wood
Falcons: American kestrel (sparrow hawk)
Finches: American goldfinch, dickcissel, house, purple

Flycatchers: eastern phoebe, eastern wood pewee, great crested, least, olive-sided, willow
Geese: Canada
Gnatcatcher: blue-gray
Goatsuckers: common nighthawk, whip-poor-will
Grebes: pied-billed
Grosbeaks: cardinal, rose-breasted
Grouse: bobwhite, ruffed
Gulls: great black-backed, herring, laughing, ring-billed
Hawks: broad-winged, Cooper's, marsh, red-shouldered, red-tailed, sharp-shinned
Herons: American bittern, black-crowned night, cattle egret, glossy ibis, great blue, great (common) egret, green, least bittern, little blue, snowy egret, yellow-crowned night

different types and, of course, swallows. In the early fall some 300,000 tree swallows swarm here before taking off in a huge flock for their vacation in the southern states and Central America.

From the end of Hanging Rock a long view of Second Beach greets us. Off in the distance on a peninsula is Sachuest Point National Wildlife Refuge. The sanctuary map shows a trail cutting through the reedy marsh from the base of this ridge to the next ridge, but all we see as we look down the face are a few red-winged blackbirds and ducks in quite undeveloped land. We retrace our steps.

Gnarled red cedars provide cover for the always exciting cardinals. Further on we pass the woodcock ''singing'' field, an open pasture with trees planted in strategic locations as cover. Each year by mid-March woodcock put on their aerial courting display here. Nearby the early migrating bobolinks pause awhile in a millet seed field planted especially for them. All these habitats provide food and cover for many varieties of birds.

This is truly a sanctuary. Not only are the birds and wildlife nurtured and protected on the grounds, but the

Hummingbirds: ruby-throated
Jays: blue
Kingbirds: eastern
Kingfishers: belted
Lark: horned
Mimics: brown thrasher, gray catbird, mockingbird
Nuthatches: white-breasted
Orioles: northern (Baltimore)
Owls: barred, great horned, screech
Oystercatcher: American (rarely)
Pheasant: ring-necked
Plovers: black-bellied, killdeer
Rails: clapper, common gallinule, king, sora, Virginia
Sandpipers: solitary, spotted
Sparrows: chipping, field, grasshopper, house, savannah, seaside, sharp-tailed, song
Starling: starling
Swallows: bank, barn, tree

Swifts: chimney
Tanagers: scarlet
Terns: black (rarely), common, Forster's (rarely), least, roseate
Thrushes: American robin, hermit, veery, wood
Towhees: rufous-sided
Vireos: red-eyed, solitary, warbling, white-eyed, yellow-throated
Vultures: turkey
Warblers: American redstart, black-and-white, ovenbird, yellow, yellowthroat
Waxwings: cedar
Woodcock: American
Woodpeckers: downy, hairy, yellow-shafted flicker
Wrens: Carolina, house, long-billed marsh, short-billed marsh

August
Norman Sanctuary

public feels free to bring the injured here, knowing they will get excellent professional care. Although we feel comfortable roaming the pathways, we know that we are only visitors; it is the animals and birds who are at home.

Long-billed marsh wrens

August
Norman Sanctuary

18 August on Lake Umbagog

[NORTHERN WOODLANDS/FRESH WATER]

Audubon Societies in both Maine and New Hampshire organize canoe trips to unspoiled Lake Umbagog to see nesting loons, ospreys, northern songbirds, marsh birds, and an occasional eagle. This wilderness lake on NH 26 out of Errol, New Hampshire, has a public launching ramp and a family campground, which is open May through September.

Our trip is in midsummer, a quiet time past the season of full-fledged songs. Most male birds sing from April to June to attract a female and indicate their territory. (Females generally chirp and call rather than sing.) Now that they have established their domain and most broods are raised, there is little need for this behavior and most songbirds confine their calls to a few scattered notes and chips. Any songs we hear now are the songs of joy.

We launch our 1923 Oldtown canoe that is a family heirloom (and a love of my life) and slip quietly away from shore. With a wooden canoe even a bump from a

August
Lake Umbagog

paddle sounds natural. The lake is barely ruffled by the breeze, and large puffy clouds decorate the surrounding mountains like Fourth of July bunting. The air is straight out of Canada: clear and cool.

Common loons swim powerfully in several coves that we pass. Known for their diving ability, they can travel great distances quickly underwater. Loons have become the symbol of primeval nature since they will not breed where they are harassed by humanity. Through our binoculars a female appears. We paddle hard to come close enough to see two young loons with their mother — a successful family this year. Loons raise only one brood of one or two chicks a year. They follow the melting ice northward to their summer nesting lakes, which are quickly becoming overpopulated with summer homes and powerboats, drastically cutting down the loon population. This view alone is worth the long ride to a northern lake.

Having secured permission earlier from the Brown Paper Company, we land on a large island and make an early camp. The fir-topped mountains of Maine and New Hampshire are mirrored in every direction. The rock-lined shore applauds each tiny wave with a gentle clap.

August
Lake Umbagog

Summer Birds
Lake Umbagog

Blackbirds: brown-headed cowbird, common grackle, red-winged, rusty
Bluebirds: eastern (rarely)
Chickadees: black-capped, boreal
Creeper: brown
Crows: common, common raven
Cuckoos: black-billed
Doves: mourning (rarely)
Ducks: black, common goldeneye, common merganser, hooded merganser, mallard (rarely), ring-necked, wood
Eagles: bald, golden
Falcons: American kestrel (sparrow hawk), peregrine (rarely)
Finches: American goldfinch, pine siskin, purple, red crossbill, white-winged crossbill

Flycatchers: alder (Traill's), eastern phoebe, eastern wood pewee, great crested, least, olive-sided, yellow-bellied
Goatsuckers: common nighthawk, whip-poor-will
Grebes: pied-billed
Grosbeaks: evening, pine, rose-breasted
Grouse: ruffed, spruce
Gulls: herring
Hawks: broad-winged, Cooper's, goshawk, marsh, red-shouldered, red-tailed, sharp-shinned
Herons: American bittern, great blue
Hummingbirds: ruby-throated
Jays: blue, gray
Kingbirds: eastern
Kingfishers: belted

Falling asleep would be easy if it weren't for the whip-poor-will. This night bird, seldom seen but often heard, calls loudly from a nearby perch. We hear a low "chuck" before the "whip." Following the sound, we walk slowly from tree to tree. Our eyes adjust to the moon and starlight, and we see quite well. A dark blob on a pale rock takes flight. The flashlight we carry is for an emergency only, and we fight the urge to flick it on.

Tiny feet patter all around us; the field mice are foraging. We hear a deep "hoo" across the water. Silent wings carry great horned owls to a quick kill. A night killer with a noiseless flight, and staring yellow eyes that never reflect the mood of the moment — no wonder Indians throughout his territory all held the great horned owl in fearful awe.

The great horned are the most powerful and courageous of our owls. They seldom build their own nests but are fierce defenders of the deserted crow and hawk nests they make their own. Mates for life, they breed early: February in southern and March in northern New England.

An hour before sunrise the early chorus begins. A distant robin is joined by a phoebe: "good morning world," and "feed me, feed me." Chipping and song

August
Lake Umbagog

Kinglets: golden-crowned, ruby-crowned
Loons: common
Mimics: brown thrasher (rarely), gray catbird
Nuthatches: red-breasted, white-breasted
Orioles: northern (Baltimore)
Osprey: osprey
Owls: barred, great horned, long-eared (rarely), saw-whet
Plovers: killdeer
Rails: sora, Virginia
Sandpipers: greater yellowlegs, solitary, spotted
Shrikes: loggerhead, northern
Snipe: common
Sparrows: chipping, dark-eyed (slate-colored) junco, Lincoln's, savannah, song, swamp, vesper, white-throated
Swallows: bank, barn, tree

Swifts: chimney
Tanagers: scarlet
Thrushes: American robin, hermit, Swainson's, veery, wood
Vireos: red-eyed, solitary, warbling
Warblers: American redstart, bay-breasted, black-and-white, Blackburnian, black-throated blue, black-throated green, Canada, Cape May, chestnut-sided, magnolia, mourning, Nashville, northern waterthrush, ovenbird, parula, Tennessee, Wilson's, yellow, yellow-rumped, yellowthroat
Waxwings: cedar
Woodcock: American
Woodpeckers: downy, hairy, yellow-bellied sapsucker, yellow-shafted flicker
Wrens: house, long-billed marsh, winter

sparrows raise their voices in homage to the sunrise; a lone hermit thrush adds his hymns to make it a choir. The phoebe's call is taken up by our stomachs. Nothing smells better in the morning on a campout than trout, bacon, eggs, and burnt toast!

We walk the shore slowly. A snipe pitters ahead of us. The snipe crouches, his streaks and stripes concealing him instantly. We stay still and he continues feeding. His long bill drills deep into the soft mud after grubs and earthworms. A snapping stick from underfoot sends him off, wings whistling, on a wildly erratic flight. His flight is much like a woodcock's.

We break camp and paddle leisurely back to the ramp, enjoying the glorious scenery. Northern New England has special meaning: clean wilderness where there is territory enough for innumerable birds — and birders.

Common loon

August
Lake Umbagog

19 September in Great Swamp

[SOUTHERN WOODLANDS/FRESH WATER]

A mile walk down a quiet tote road is the forest entrance to Great Swamp — two habitats in one. The way to Great Swamp Management Area, off RI 138 in West Kingston, Rhode Island, is well marked. A walk here in September brings us to migrating songbirds and water birds, in addition to the summer residents who have not yet left.

We pass black swamp water where mosquitoes still buzz. In the distance a train's whistle sounds, then a school band starts practicing for a football half-time show, and finally, we hear a crow of the state bird, the Rhode Island red rooster: sounds of our culture in microcosm.

A tufted titmouse hops to the road from a low-hanging pin oak branch, picks up some small seeds, and then flies to a puddle for a quick bath. This gray, chunky, chickadee-sized bird with an ever-present crest is an energetic bundle of feathers.

A power line runs down a hill through the trees and across the swamp. We listen to an indigo bunting singing from this field environment. He is one of the few songbirds who continue to sing during this season. As the light changes, the color of this bird who represents his tropical family here in the North country appears green, teal blue, pale green, and then indigo.

A rich-looking alfalfa field returns nutrients to the soil along the side of the road. Ahead we see dark forms scrabbling in the dirt — a family of bobwhites. The chicks are almost as large as their parents, but they still wait for their elders' signal before they flush at our approach. They fly only two feet before settling back to the edge of the woods in the grasses. We can hear them peeping as we step closer, but their camouflage is complete, and we don't see them until they whirl up from underfoot like the dry leaves in a fall breeze.

We leave the power-line road and make our way to the right down the dike road around Great Swamp (none of these roads is blazed). Open water separates the dike from hummocks of grass and reeds in which an occasional swamp maple anchors its roots. Every one hundred feet or so a wood duck box hangs on a pole. Never have we seen so many boxes in one area. In a small cove we see several "woodies" dipping. A male in eclipse (fall) plumage preens himself on a half-

September
Great Swamp

Early Fall

Great Swamp

Blackbirds: brown-headed cowbird, common grackle, eastern meadowlark, red-winged
Bluebirds: eastern
Buntings: indigo
Chickadees: black-capped, tufted titmouse
Creeper: brown
Crows: common
Cuckoos: black-billed, yellow-billed
Doves: mourning
Ducks: black, mallard, northern shoveler, wood
Falcons: American kestrel (sparrow hawk)

Finches: American goldfinch, dickcissel, house, purple
Flycatchers: alder (Traill's), eastern phoebe, eastern wood pewee, great crested, least, olive-sided, willow, yellow-bellied
Geese: Canada
Goatsuckers: common nighthawk, whip-poor-will
Grosbeaks: cardinal, rose-breasted
Grouse: bobwhite, ruffed
Hawks: broad-winged, Cooper's, marsh, red-shouldered, red-tailed, sharp-shinned
Herons: American bittern, black-crowned night, great blue, green, yellow-crowned night
Hummingbirds: ruby-throated
Jays: blue
Kingbirds: eastern
Kingfishers: belted

submerged log. Penguins wear tuxedos; wood ducks wear flashy sport coats. By the time we walk halfway around the marsh we know that the wood duck propagation program is successful. We count eighty-four in the late afternoon sky.

Deep holes dug along the dike path are littered with the remains of eggshells. A fox or skunk has found the nests of snapping turtles. The eggshells are leathery to the touch, quite unlike those of a bird. We applaud the marauder, for this turtle feeds on the swimming young of ducks and geese.

Beneath a tall tree along the dike we find the remains of an owl dinner: an owl pellet. Pulling this small package apart, we find the undigested parts of a mouse: fur, teeth, and skull. Other pellets litter the ground. This must be a favorite roost.

A partially sunken boardwalk provides us with a way closer to an osprey nest, one of the most spectacular sights here in Great Swamp. Built on man-made platforms, on the power-line poles, and in the branches of a dead maple, these huge stick nests seem to be everywhere. This marsh is one of the best places in all of New England to see such a colony.

An osprey is an awesome sight as it plunges fifty feet into water after a perch or pickerel: a graceful glide on wings almost as long as an eagle's though less broad, a

Lark: horned
Mimics: brown thrasher, gray catbird, mockingbird
Nuthatches: red-breasted, white-breasted
Orioles: northern (Baltimore)
Osprey: osprey
Owls: barred, great horned, long-eared, screech
Pheasant: ring-necked
Plovers: killdeer, semipalmated
Rails: American coot, clapper, common gallinule, sora, Virginia
Sandpipers: solitary, spotted
Sparrows: chipping, dark-eyed (slate-colored) junco, field, grasshopper, house, savannah, sharp-tailed, song, swamp, vesper, white-throated
Starling: starling

Swallows: barn, tree
Swifts: chimney
Tanagers: scarlet
Thrushes: American robin, gray-cheeked, hermit, Swainson's, veery, wood
Towhees: rufous-sided
Vireos: Philadelphia, red-eyed, solitary, warbling, white-eyed, yellow-throated
Vultures: turkey
Warblers: (many on migration)
Waxwings: cedar
Woodcock: American
Woodpeckers: downy, hairy, pileated, red-headed, yellow-bellied sapsucker, yellow-shafted flicker
Wrens: Carolina, house, long-billed marsh, short-billed marsh, winter

September
Great Swamp

brief hover as he eyes a fish near the surface, a folding of wings, and then a mighty splash. Often a songbird will build its nest within the layers of an osprey nest. Since the osprey drives off hawks that might prey on its young, the smaller bird is safe in this fish-lover's domain.

To help the osprey population make a comeback after it was nearly decimated by DDT, Fish and Game officials in many states raided ospreys' nests and carried off recently laid eggs to be hatched in incubators. The chicks were hand-raised and then returned to the wild. When the female osprey discovered an egg was missing, she laid another in its place, so three to five chicks were born each breeding season rather than the usual two to four. If the similar bald eagle program were as successful, the national symbol would be once more in the public's eye.

As evening colors the sky, the muted tones are reflected in dark swamp water. The silent flight of an owl passes eerily across the picture. We quietly make our way back through the dim woods.

September
Great Swamp

Great horned owl

20 September at Quechee Gorge

[NORTHERN WOODLANDS]

The water is low now in Quechee Gorge. In spring when it thunders out of Vermont's Quechee Lakes into the 163-foot-deep chasm bird songs are lost within its voice. Early September offers a less spectacular backdrop for a bird walk, but as we walk beneath the bridge carrying US 4, we are able to hear "phwee-be" over the sound of tumbling water.

A grayish-olive phoebe has built a nest and raised three broods this hot year. So tame are these gentle birds that they often build in spots that are awkward for people, such as door ledges. They return for several years to the same familiar nest, building layer upon layer. This typical flycatcher's song is a nasal "phwee-be," a fuller sound than the "fee-bee" of the black-capped chickadee, who shares the same woods habitat. Although it looks to the beginner as though the wood pewee's "pee-wee" might be confused easily

September
Quechee Gorge

87

with the phoebe's and the chickadee's calls, its song is a thin whistle with a downward lilt to the first half that sounds distinctive. Identifying bird songs is indeed an art.

We walk down the steep hemlock-lined road, listening for the white-throated sparrow's "da, da, dee dee dee," which is interpreted in field guides as "old Sam Peabody." That rustling of dry leaves just off the path might be one scratching. Now that the molt of feathers is over, the white-throated sparrows are slowly moving south in groups of several families.

Suddenly the booming of water in the gorge takes on a new depth. We feel a thumping sound resonating on our chests as of a distant tractor starting up. A male ruffed grouse is drumming to challenge a rival. The drumming sound is caused by sudden blows on the air, rather than by the wings hitting each other or the hollow log on which he displays. We hope his female is as impressed as we are.

We reach the bottom of an incline where a bog

September
Quechee Gorge

Early Fall Birds
Quechee Gorge

Blackbirds: common grackle, red-winged
Chickadees: black-capped
Creeper: brown
Crows: common
Cuckoos: black-billed
Falcons: American kestrel (sparrow hawk)
Finches: American goldfinch, pine siskin, purple
Flycatchers: alder (Traill's), eastern phoebe, eastern wood pewee, great crested, least, olive-sided
Goatsuckers: common nighthawk, whip-poor-will
Grosbeaks: rose-breasted
Grouse: ruffed
Hawks: broad-winged, red-shouldered, red-tailed, sharp-shinned
Herons: American bittern, great blue, green
Hummingbirds: ruby-throated
Jays: blue
Kingbirds: eastern
Kingfishers: belted

Kinglets: golden-crowned, ruby-crowned
Mimics: brown thrasher, gray catbird
Nuthatches: red-breasted, white-breasted
Orioles: northern (Baltimore)
Owls: barred, great horned, long-eared
Plovers: killdeer
Sandpipers: spotted
Snipe: common
Sparrows: dark-eyed (slate-colored) junco, field, house, Lincoln's, song, swamp, white-throated
Starling: starling
Swallows: tree
Tanagers: scarlet
Thrushes: American robin, hermit, Swainson's, veery, wood
Towhees: rufous-sided
Vireos: Philadelphia, red-eyed, solitary, warbling
Warblers: (many on migration)
Waxwings: cedar
Woodcock: American
Woodpeckers: downy, hairy, yellow-bellied sapsucker, yellow-shafted flicker
Wrens: house, winter

nestles to the left of the road. Small blue dragonflies whir their helicopter wings, skimming the algae-covered pond. A red-winged blackbird sits in an alder bush nearby, occasionally dashing off after a snack.

Atop red sumac berries a catbird meows. These berries, not the white, itch-producing poisonous kind, provide nourishment for both men and birds. They are recommended for planting as winter bird food, although Russian olive seems to be a preferred berry. Easy to grow in the poorest soil, they have scarlet leaves that look like poinsettias in the fall. The berries when mashed in water, strained, and then sweetened, make a delicious sumac-ade. Local Indians stored the berries for their winter use, knowing the benefit of fruit in their diet.

We follow the Ottauquechee River past the base of the gorge where the countryside opens out. An islet with dead pines covered with grapevines splits the river. Binoculars are made for this opportunity. We sit at the meadow's fringe bracing our elbows on our knees, and scan the island. A spotted sandpiper wags his tail along the edge of the water. A robin eats grapes. A kingfisher waits on an overhanging branch.

The meadow waves its flower fingers. Asters are everywhere. Milkweed is thick. Some monarch butterflies flit, while others form in their "zippered" chrysalis beneath the dry, curled milkweed leaves. We hope the latter complete their metamorphosis before the first killing frost. Purple polka dots spot the yellowing green; from thistle to thistle goldfinches fly their unique oscillating flight to their favorite seeds. At this season many males have not yet lost their black caps and brilliant lemon yellow feathers, although some are molting and will shortly be in gray green plumage. We can identify them any time of the year though by the undulating flight and the matching chipping song. The "wild canary" of the north is late nesting, fun-loving, and always singing.

Returning from the warm sunny meadow to the cool, dim dampness of the gorge, we see a female black-and-white warbler "nuthatching" her way head-first

September
Quechee Gorge

89

down a rough pitch pine. She has the black head stripes of the male but not the black cheeks. This warbler is both common and easy to see since it finds its food in tree bark, not on the wing.

Two children splash in a private basin in the river, the bridge high above. Swallows whip up a gentle breeze over them — the last of summer.

September
Quechee Gorge

Ruffed grouse

21 October in Wachusett Meadows

[SOUTHERN WOODLANDS]

Come early October the color line of fall foliage advances to southern New England. Trees are lighting up. Wachusett Meadows Wildlife Sanctuary, located just west of Princeton, Massachusetts off MA 62 on the Goodnow Road, is beautiful for birds *and* birders.

We walk from the parking lot down a hill through the dry grasses of a large field, startling sparrows along the way. We think of sparrows as being plain of color, plain of song, and plain of habit, but in fact they have intricate feather patterns and elaborate songs.

At the bottom of the field a boardwalk begins its winding way through the tree-dimmed swamp. Just as we enter the woods on the sturdy plank walk, a black-billed cuckoo clucks. Unlike its European counterpart, it doesn't call "cuckoo" as in the famous clock; it simply calls the first half, "kook, kook, kook." (This sounds to me like two wooden blocks hit together as in

October

Wachusett Meadows

Leroy Anderson's tune "Sleigh Ride.") The black-billed cuckoo has become much more common in New England in the past few years because of the influx of tent caterpillars, its favorite food. When the tent caterpillar population declines, however, so does the number of black-billed cuckoos.

A warbling vireo catches a caterpillar, then a fly, and then another caterpillar. This beneficial bird is seen less often now than in years past. Its niche has been taken over by the more aggressive import, the house sparrow. A lovely song pours out of him from April to September, which is longer than most birds sing. He even sings while sitting on the nest, a characteristic of all male vireos.

The boardwalk winds on through the swamp. An algae-covered brook provides a brief opening to the sky. Darning needles of red, purple, blue, and green skim the lilypads. Spotted turtles sun on a warm bank. Cedar waxwings, always a small surprise, flit through the alders. Warblers on their way south make gentle chickadeelike squeaks as they move from tree to tree. A yellowthroat is a pale reminder of the brilliance of spring warblers, but his mask still gives him away.

The remnants of a pitcher plant squat in a muddy spot near enough to the walk for us to see the flies caught deep in the "pitcher." This carnivorous plant has not only interesting eating habits but the strangest looking

October
Wachusett Meadows

Fall Birds

Wachusett Meadows

Blackbirds: brown-headed cowbird, common grackle, eastern meadowlark, red-winged
Bluebirds: eastern
Chickadees: black-capped, tufted titmouse
Creeper: brown
Crows: common
Cuckoos: black-billed
Doves: mourning
Ducks: black, mallard, wood
Falcons: American kestrel (sparrow hawk)
Finches: American goldfinch, purple

Flycatchers: alder (Traill's), eastern phoebe, eastern wood pewee, great crested, least
Geese: Canada
Goatsuckers: common nighthawk, whip-poor-will
Grosbeaks: cardinal, evening, rose-breasted
Grouse: ruffed
Hawks: broad-winged, Cooper's, goshawk, red-shouldered, red-tailed, sharp-shinned
Herons: American bittern, black-crowned night, great blue, green
Hummingbirds: ruby-throated

blossom we've come across. The boardwalk here certainly opens new territory for us.

We step off the boardwalk onto the slick needle carpet of a white pine grove. Evidence of pileated woodpeckers is everywhere: holes drilled two feet long and five inches wide. A screaming cry alerts us to the pileated. The sound is much like that of the yellow-shafted flicker. This woodpecker, which reminds us of the pterodactyl, is remarkably shy. We lie on the sweet smelling pine needles and wait. Crashing through the dead limbs of the pines, he beats towards his favorite holey tree but departs in a hurry when he spies us. His noisy exit leaves red squirrels chattering.

We follow the trail back to the parking lot. A view over the pond below the picnic area reveals two circling sharp-shinned hawks. The resident naturalist tells us that they have been here all summer and have nested. Once a pair of hawks has established a nesting site, it tends to return every year, if it is not bothered. Perhaps this is the beginning of their migration. The ponds themselves are empty of the resident ducks, although occasional flocks of migrating ducks do hit these ponds during the fall.

Across the road another set of trails winds through dry uplands. We pass many bluebird houses next to the farmhouse. Ten pairs raised families here this summer. The rough-winged and cliff swallows are long gone, as

Jays: blue
Kingbirds: eastern
Kingfishers: belted
Kinglets: golden-crowned, ruby-crowned
Mimics: brown thrasher, gray catbird, mockingbird
Nuthatches: red-breasted, white-breasted
Orioles: northern (Baltimore), orchard
Owls: barred, great horned, screech
Pheasant: ring-necked
Plovers: killdeer
Rails: king, Virginia
Snipe: common
Sparrows: chipping, dark-eyed (slate-colored) junco, field, house, song, swamp, tree, white-throated
Starling: starling
Swifts: chimney
Tanagers: scarlet
Towhees: rufous-sided
Vireos: Philadelphia, red-eyed, solitary, warbling
Vultures: turkey
Warblers: (many on migration)
Waxwings: cedar
Woodcock: American
Woodpeckers: downy, hairy, pileated, yellow-bellied sapsucker, yellow-shafted flicker
Wrens: house

October
Wachusett Meadows

are the bobolinks. At the side of the bobolink field we spot the massive Crocker Maple. Although we know it to be the fourth largest sugar maple in the country, we are still stunned by its size.

The lemon yellow of newly colored trees dapples our path toward a large glacial boulder. Highlighted on this gray rock is an oddly colored bird: spattered yellow, green, red, and black feathers in little pattern bedeck a scarlet tanager in fall plumage. The rich purple of an oak branch adds even more color to the sight. This common woodland bird hides in dense foliage, and it is an event when we spot him.

As we walk back toward the car I think that the red of a single scarlet tanager feather would go well on my hat with the lovely blue jay feather collected after the August molting season . . . never found one, though.

Pileated woodpeckers

October
Wachusett Meadows

22 October Atop Mount Greylock

[NORTHERN WOODLANDS/SOUTHERN WOODLANDS]

The newly paved road from North Adams to the top of Mount Greylock adds easy accessibility to this highest point in Massachusetts. The road winds and turns back on itself, offering broad views of the Berkshire's fall foliage. A primitive, beautiful campground is located near the summit. Miles of trails, including the Appalachian, pass over this peak, nearly all of them running through dense woods. Perfect for the gray-cheeked thrush's most southerly nesting place, they do *not* offer the sky views we need for hawk watching, our main purpose today.

After breakfasting in style at one of the lean-tos, we head over to the open picnic grounds. The wide view is north-northeast into the ''Hopper,'' a large natural fold that funnels northwest winds up and over the mountain. It is a perfect place to see migrating hawks.

October
Mount Greylock

95

Hawks are generally loners. Their territorial needs are great, since they are at the top of the bird food chain. At this time of year they migrate together in loose groups, so if the weather conditions are right we can see hundreds of hawks in one day.

Today is such a day. In the bright sunshine specks float slowly across the line of vision. A good breeze is blowing, and we watch sharp-shinned hawks on their way south. They circle, gain altitude, and coast down the current.

The sharp-shinned hawk is bold, sometimes attacking a bird larger than itself, including full-grown poultry. He has even been known to chase an osprey during the breeding season. Unlike other hawks, this bird builds a neat nest of woven sticks sometimes only twenty feet from the ground. The usual hawk nest is a loose bundle of sticks high in a tree. Both parents have to work hard feeding their one brood, as it takes three or four small birds daily to satisfy a large nestling.

The yellow birches flicker in the breeze as we drain our thermos of coffee, enjoying the view. We return to the campground where we pick up the Hopper Trail and then the Overlook Trail to the peak of the 3,491-foot-high mountain. As we cross the road we notice a tiny gray hawklike bird sitting atop a fence post, surveying

Fall Birds
Mount Greylock

Chickadees: black-capped
Creeper: brown
Crows: common
Falcons: American kestrel (sparrow hawk)
Finches: American goldfinch, pine siskin, purple, red crossbill
Flycatchers: eastern phoebe
Grosbeaks: pine
Grouse: ruffed
Hawks: broad-winged, Cooper's, goshawk, marsh, red-shouldered, red-tailed, rough-legged, sharp-shinned
Jays: blue
Kinglets: golden-crowned, ruby-crowned
Mimics: brown thrasher

Nuthatches: red-breasted, white-breasted
Owls: barred, great horned, long-eared, screech
Shrikes: northern (rarely)
Sparrows: chipping, dark-eyed (slate-colored) junco, fox, song, tree, white-crowned, white-throated
Swallows: tree
Thrushes: American robin, gray-cheeked, hermit, Swainson's
Towhees: rufous-sided
Vireos: red-eyed, solitary
Woodcock: American
Woodpeckers: black-backed three-toed, downy, hairy, yellow-bellied sapsucker, yellow-shafted flicker
Wrens: house, winter

October

Mount Greylock

the valley below. The shrill note, resembling a child's whistle, jars us as the shrike launches into the air. He is on the attack! A large moth makes the mistake of flying by at the wrong moment and is no more.

The shrike's feeding habits have caused him to be nicknamed the "butcher bird." At times he will attack a flock of birds, drive one to the ground, kill it, and hang it on a barbed-wire fence or convenient thorn bush for a delayed dinner. A rare bird to these parts, we are delighted to see him.

At the top of Mount Greylock a war memorial with fresh flowers recalls harsher times. The wind blows chilly; there are few trees at the summit for protection. Looking back toward the "Hopper" we see a few broad-winged hawks "kettling." They have been flying low, probably from the nearby valley woods, and are now gaining altitude with wings outstretched, every finger showing. They are circling round and round an invisible spiral staircase of wind only thirty feet wide: a visible sign of a thermal. It reminds us of the memorial's steps behind us.

The broad-winged is one of the tamest and easiest hawks to identify. The trick to identifying hawks is to memorize their silhouettes, taking note of the shape and size of the wings and tail. When we walk a woods road we might see an occasional perched hawk, but the usual view is a dark outline against the sky.

Along with the small birds at the greatest time of migration, the Cooper's hawk flies. This hawk isn't as likely to be seen as the red-shouldered or red-tailed hawks who sail more conspicuously. He is both swift and powerful enough to kill rabbits, though his diet is comprised largely of birds.

We identify some red-tailed hawks soaring literally through the clouds. An interruption in the flight! Tumbling toward the ground are two battering each other with wings and clutching at torn feathers with talons. They level off just short of the parking lot and swoop over the cliff. The motive today is obscure for such a battle.

The small falcon, the kestrel, sometimes migrates

October
Mount Greylock

97

too, though we haven't been lucky enough to see one today. They are the hovering hawks seen over meadows. When they winter over, as many do, they have a hard time of it, since their main diet is insects.

Far above more hawks sail by. Oh, to be a glider pilot today!

Red-tailed hawks

October
Mount Greylock

23 October on Block Island

[SOUTHERN COAST/ATLANTIC FLYWAY]

The ferry *Quonset* takes us across to Block Island from Point Judith, Rhode Island, on the tail of a strong northwest wind. Small craft warnings prepare us for the twelve-mile roller coaster ride.

The Atlantic flyway is the shore route for the migrating birds. Often strong winds blow the immatures out to sea, drowning thousands who have become lost. Since it is the first trip for many birds, their lack of experience leads them to ride an easy wind, rather than wait the bad weather out. Block Island has tall bluffs, and many lost birds head toward it after being blown off course, where they land exhausted. After winds like we've just had, we can walk up to those fall warblers that are so hard to identify in their usual flickering flight.

After dropping our overnight bags at a lovely inn that seems exclusively filled with birders, we walk the coast road. Low bushes of bayberry, wild rose, beach plum, sweetpea, and honeysuckle overpower us with their glorious unfrosted scents. Warblers sit remarkably still

October
Block Island

throughout the underbrush. The sand cliffs of the island fall away from our feet as we gaze down Mohegan Bluffs. We are a couple of hundred feet high here on the southeast coast.

Continuing on our circuit, we see a great blue heron working his way around the the edge of a small pond. Two mute swans lend grace to the scene. An American coot slips under the dark water. A slate gray duck-sized bird, the coot's conspicuous white bill distinguishes it from ducks, with which it often feeds. There can be nothing in the bird world that looks sillier to the human beholder than a coot running along the surface of the water as he prepares to take off.

We walk back to the hotel near the ferry landing. Booming surf hypnotizes us to sleep.

Early the next morning we rent bicycles to head to the north point and Sachem Pond Wildlife Sanctuary. The Atlantic rolls placidly onto Crescent Beach this bright day. Sandpipers play tag with the low breakers as herring gulls scavenge at the high-water line of seaweed.

We pass New Harbor on our left and spot Canada

Fall Birds
Block Island

Blackbirds: brown-headed cowbird, common grackle, eastern meadowlark, red-winged, rusty
Bluebirds: eastern
Buntings: indigo, snow
Chickadees: black-capped, tufted titmouse
Cormorants: double-crested, great
Creeper: brown
Crows: common, fish
Cuckoos: black-billed, yellow-billed
Doves: mourning, rock (pigeon)
Ducks: American wigeon, black, blue-winged teal, bufflehead, canvasback, common goldeneye, gadwall, greater scaup, green-winged teal, hooded merganser, lesser scaup, mallard, northern shoveler, pintail, red-breasted merganser, redhead, ring-necked, ruddy, scoters, wood

Eagles: bald, golden
Falcons: American kestrel (sparrow hawk), merlin (pigeon hawk), peregrine
Finches: American goldfinch, dickcissel, house, pine siskin, purple
Flycatchers: eastern phoebe
Geese: brant, Canada, snow (blue)
Gnatcatcher: blue-gray
Goatsuckers: common nighthawk, whip-poor-will
Grebes: horned, pied-billed, red-necked
Grosbeaks: cardinal, evening
Grouse: bobwhite, ruffed
Gulls: Bonaparte's, great black-backed, herring, laughing, ring-billed
Hawks: marsh, red-shouldered, red-tailed, sharp-shinned
Herons: American bittern, black-crowned night, cattle egret, great blue, great (common) egret, green, snowy egret, yellow-crowned night

October
Block Island

geese resting in the deep salt water harbor. A snowy egret wades in the marsh as sparrows flit in the dry grasses. A marsh hawk hovers just above the bushtops (there are few trees other than settler-planted apples and pears), drops into the brush, and then appears again to glide out of sight.

High on Bush Hill we smell the delicious aroma of apples. The drops make a tart treat as we scan the fields below with our binoculars. A rufous-sided towhee lets us know he is near with his thunderous scratching. Towhees are a usual "starter bird" for beginning birders. They rustle through the dead leaves looking for insects and seeds. The male has a black hood, cowl, and cape, chestnut orange sides, a white breast, and white outer tail feathers. His fancy coloring and noisy eating habits make him quite conspicuous and therefore easy to identify. We admire the plain "Quaker dress" of the demure female as she darts under a bush. A farm field yields the sight of a magnificent cock pheasant striding along a stone wall. Grazing sheep complete the pastoral scene.

Coasting down Corn Neck Road, we come quickly to

Jays: blue
Kingfishers: belted
Kinglets: golden-crowned, ruby-crowned
Lark: horned
Loons: common, red-throated
Mimics: mockingbird
Nuthatches: red breasted, white-breasted
Orioles: northern (Baltimore)
Osprey: osprey
Owls: barn, great-horned, long-eared, screech, short-eared
Pipits: water
Pheasant: ring-necked
Plovers: black-bellied, killdeer, semipalmated
Rails: American coot, clapper, common gallinule, sora, Virginia
Sandpipers: dunlin, greater yellowlegs, least, lesser yellowlegs, pectoral, purple, sanderling, semipalmated, solitary, spotted, western white-rumped

Shrikes: loggerhead
Snipe: common
Sparrows: chipping, dark-eyed (slate-colored) junco, field, fox, grasshopper, house, Lapland longspur, savannah, seaside, sharp-tailed, song, swamp, tree, vesper, white-crowned, white-throated
Starling: starling
Swallows: tree
Swan: mute
Tanagers: scarlet
Thrushes: American robin, hermit
Towhees: rufous-sided
Vireos: red-eyed, solitary
Warblers: (many during migration)
Waxwings: cedar
Woodcock: American
Woodpeckers: downy, hairy, yellow-shafted flicker
Wrens: Carolina, house, long-billed marsh, short-billed marsh, winter

October

Block Island

the sanctuary. The north end of Block Island is the "jumping off" place for all the sea-swept birds returning to the mainland coastline to continue their migration. Sandy Point is covered with birds. As a belted kingfisher flashes his spear-head down through the air in an unsuccessful dive, two immature snow geese ride proudly on the sun-rippled pond at the refuge. These dark geese with their gray bills will return in the spring after another molt with many more white feathers. We hope that they find a flock to join on their journey south: two would make a poor **V** in the sky.

Ducks dot the pond — blacks, mallards, and teal. A flock of large red-necked grebes bobs up like apples at a Halloween party. Although much smaller than loons, their silhouettes in the water are similar.

The shore of Rhode Island is blue in the distance as we walk out the sandbar. Sandpipers zip just above the waves so quickly we are unable to focus our binoculars on them. A short wade convinces us that winter is near.

We pedal back to the hotel, catching sight of many kinds of warblers working their way to the point. As we make the twelve-mile run to the mainland, a flock of warblers easily passes us. The brief stopover on Block Island has renewed both them and us.

Rufous-sided towhee

October
Block Island

24 November in Larsen Sanctuary

[SOUTHERN SUBURBS]

The Connecticut Audubon Society headquarters is located at Larsen Sanctuary on Burr St. in Fairfield, Connecticut. The 170-acre nature preserve with 6½ miles of trails is a gentle wilderness in the suburbs. A "Singing and Fragrance Walk" for the blind begins next to the parking lot. This smooth path with wood rails has special plantings of heavily scented bushes and flowers, although we are too late to enjoy their smell. There are other such walks throughout New England. State park systems and Audubon societies have the addresses. Bird songs make up such a large part of birding that this activity is a joy for the blind.

It is a cool, cloudy, early November day, not the kind of day most people enjoy being outdoors. The sanctuary paths are empty of people, but the birds are still here. Some are late migrants; others are permanent residents.

A red-eyed vireo sings his robinlike phrases. He sits on a low branch, slowly turning his head to examine each leaf. Singing all the while, he flits to a bush which bends beneath him. He has grabbed a green caterpillar, his usual food. The upward pitch of his final note adds a question to his song as he warbles again. We wonder why he didn't leave New England earlier with the rest of his kind.

A night migrant, the red-eyed vireo travels south with flocks of flycatchers, sparrows, thrushes, orioles, and warblers by the light of the stars. While I was writing at my desk late one night with windows wide open, a red-eyed vireo flew in. After much fuss, he settled on top of a doorway while I tried to decide how to get him back outside. Finally I threw a sheet over him, trapping him beneath. As I released that fluff of heartbeats, the whir of many wings and the quiet chirps from many birds above told me that a large flock was passing through.

Night is a safer time for the small birds to travel than the predator-filled days. In past years we have set up a small telescope in our backyard during late September or early October (migration is early in New Hampshire). Pointing it at the full moon, we have watched myriad songbirds pass by. They are invisible to our naked eyes, flying hundreds of feet high over obstacles.

The whisper song of a robin comes from a low branch of a maple by the path. A much quieter replica of the spring "cheerup, cheerie," it is sung from midsummer through fall. Although he is only a few feet away, his song sounds like a tiny bird's imitation from a hundred feet away. The robin is the state bird of Connecticut. Surely it is the most looked-for thrush in March and the most over-looked after April. Many spend the winter in New England, feeding on barberry, rose hips, and hawthorn or ash berries.

A bell-like series of notes echoes through the tunnel of maples in which we are walking. It is so unlike the

November

Larsen Sanctuary

usual sound that comes from the handsome blue jay. Blue jays are voracious eaters, as any bird feeder attests after their half hour "snacks." They store many of the seeds in nooks and crannies of bark for later feedings. Their blue plumage brightens the winter days of New England, whether you are snowshoeing in Maine's Baxter Park or throwing bread crumbs out of a Connecticut apartment window.

The woodchip-lined path is soft to the feet, dampening any sounds we make as we sneak up on birds. Remembering that smooth, slow movement is accepted as "nothing dangerous," we move to an opening by one of the ponds. A swamp sparrow walks about on the mud under some grasses picking at weed seeds. Happier away from human company, he is one of the less commonly seen sparrows.

An empty wood duck box sits atop a pole in the middle of the pond. Wood ducks used to nest in old woodpecker holes in dead trees above water. To increase the possible nesting places, fish and game clubs, state game departments, and interested private citizens erect these nesting boxes. We have watched this spectacularly beautiful bird preen himself at different locales throughout New England. This preening cleans and oils his feathers — a necessary job, not vanity. Although maintaining a wood duck box is work, the sight of this bird is worth it.

Fall Birds
Larsen Sanctuary

Chickadees: black-capped, tufted titmouse
Crows: common
Doves: mourning, rock (pigeon)
Ducks: wood
Finches: American goldfinch, house, pine siskin
Gnatcatcher: blue-gray
Goatsuckers: common nighthawk
Grosbeaks: cardinal
Hummingbirds: ruby-throated
Jays: blue
Kingfishers: belted
Kinglets: golden-crowned, ruby-crowned

Mimics: mockingbird
Nuthatches: white-breasted
Sparrows: chipping, dark-eyed (slate-colored) junco, field, fox, house, savannah, song, swamp, tree, white-throated
Starling: starling
Swallows: barn, tree
Swifts: chimney
Thrushes: robin, veery, wood
Towhees: rufous-sided
Vireos: red-eyed, warbling, white-eyed, yellow-throated
Warblers: (many on migration)
Waxwings: cedar
Woodpeckers: downy, yellow-shafted flicker
Wrens: house

November
Larsen Sanctuary

An ovenbird runs across the path as we turn to leave
— such a friendly little warbler. He is very late on his
migration. He flips a farewell with his tail and is gone.

Blue jay

November
Larsen Sanctuary

25 December on a Christmas Count

[ALL NEW ENGLAND HABITATS]

Toward the year's end, the great earth paperweight shakes itself, and it begins to snow on New England. Fat, fluffy flakes drift down on the bare frozen ground, quickly covering it. The birds flock to windowsill feeders to stock up (knowing in their bones that a storm is brewing). In December Audubon societies throughout the country organize experienced birders into groups for a "Christmas Count." We join the Coast Count in New Hampshire. Beginners are welcome as hangers-on only since mistaken identity of a bird is taken seriously.

A circle with a fifteen-mile radius has been laid out. We are to list every bird seen or heard within this area this weekend. People have been calling the Audubon Society to tell of interesting birds they have seen in the area or at their feeders, so we have a few clues on where to start our count.

We drive to a marsh overlook, set up a scope, and let the experts go to work. The winter plumage is confusing, since it is such a washed-out version of the breeding plumage. Lapland longspurs run on the wind-swept ground near the parking lot — a good find for this count.

Far to the right a peninsula juts into the marsh. What appears to be a white plastic bag caught in the brush becomes a snowy owl when our binoculars find it. He is an example of an "incursive" species: one we seldom see unless he is driven here by fierce weather or by lack of food on his home territory. Besides this owl, we might see a rough-legged hawk, a flock of common redpolls, or perhaps some Bohemian waxwings.

We jump back into our car cavalcade and head off to a backyard feeding station where a gray jay has been calling all week. He is not here today — common luck for the birder. Perhaps it was a case of mistaken identity — we do see a shrike — as gray jays are extremely rare this far south. Our disappointment shrinks as we are offered hot coffee and freshly baked Christmas cookies. Evening grosbeaks and chickadees attack the sunflower seed, millet seed, and cracked corn mixture hanging outside while we enjoy our refreshments inside. A downy woodpecker picks at a suet ball.

Further into the day, we stop in a small woods. A black stream cuts through the white snow. We listen. The quiet chips of chickadees are broken by the harsh voice of a crow and the rhythmic tatoo of a woodpecker. We push through the snow (which always seems deeper in the woods) and find a yellow-bellied sapsucker who is wintering over.

Although the unusual bird adds spice to our hunt, all birds are counted. A study of the Christmas Counts in the National Audubon Society's *American Birds* shows precise population fluctuations and territory extensions.

One of the more noteworthy facts gleaned from these counts is the recent "explosion" northward of the mockingbirds. For 1973 New Hampshire listed only seventeen sightings in the state over the entire year. There must have been that many nesting pairs in the city of Rochester alone in 1977.

Our group moves on to the coast, while others continue counting inland. We set up the scope again and scan the waves. The uncommon common scoter floats in a scattered flock. The expected goldeneyes, old-squaws, and loons dot the oceanscape. We feel heroic braving the cold today, but this freezing weather out in the open is normal for these birds. We decide, ''enough is enough,'' and head home. As we drive into the yard, a cardinal turns our snow-decked pine into a Christmas card picture.

Audubon societies have much more to offer than just Christmas Counts. One of their aims is to promote birding, so many of their programs are designed specifically for the neophyte. By contacting the Audubon society in your state, you can get lists of sanctuaries and birds by season and abundance, information about organized field trips, general birding activities, and, of course, conservation efforts in your area.

Maine Audubon Society
Gilsland Farm
Old Route 1
Falmouth, Maine 04105

Connecticut Audubon Society
2325 Burr Street
Fairfield, Connecticut 06430

Massachusetts Audubon Society
Lincoln, Massachusetts 01773

Audubon Society of New Hampshire
Silk Farm Road
Concord, New Hampshire 03301

December
Christmas Count

Audubon Society of Rhode Island
40 Bowen Street
Providence, Rhode Island 02903

Vermont Audubon Society
P.O. Box 33
Burlington, Vermont 05401

Cardinal

December
Christmas Count

Appendix: Other Field Trips in New England

I. Northern Woodlands
   a. Moosehorn National Wildlife Refuge. . .Maine
   b. Bangor Bog. . .Maine
   c. Tuckerman Ravine. . .New Hampshire
   d. Kancamagus Highway Trails. . .New Hampshire
   e. Elmore State Park. . .Vermont
   f. Lake Saint Catherine State Park. . .Vermont
II. Northern Coast
   a. Rachel Carson Sanctuary. . .Maine
   b. Biddeford Pool. . .Maine
   c. Acadia National Park. . .Maine
   d. Odiorne State Park. . .New Hampshire
   e. Newburyport. . .Massachusetts
   f. Cape Ann. . .Massachusetts
III. Northern Fresh Water
   a. Moosehead Lake. . .Maine
   b. Allagash Waterway. . .Maine
   c. Merrymeeting Marsh. . .New Hampshire
   d. Connecticut Lakes. . .New Hampshire
   e. Connecticut River. . .New Hampshire, Vermont
   f. DAR State Park. . .Vermont
IV. Southern Woodlands
   a. Kimball Sanctuary. . .Rhode Island
   b. Pulaski Memorial State Park. . .Rhode Island
   c. Pachaug State Forest. . .Connecticut
   d. Nipmuck Trail. . .Connecticut
   e. Arcadia Sanctuary. . .Massachusetts
   f. Stony Brook Sanctuary. . .Massachusetts
V. Southern Coast
   a. Point Judith. . .Rhode Island
   b. Goddard Memorial State Park. . .Rhode Island
   c. Rocky Neck State Park. . .Connecticut
   e. Martha's Vineyard. . .Massachusetts

f. Cape Cod National Seashore. . .Massachusetts

VI. Southern Fresh Water

  a. Connecticut River. . .Massachusetts,
      Connecticut

  b. Burlingame State Park. . .Rhode Island

  c. Ipswich River. . .Massachusetts

VII. City

  a. Mount Auburn Cemetery. . .Boston,
      Massachusetts

  b. Baxter Boulevard. . .Portland, Maine

Index

Page numbers in **boldface** type indicate an illustration.